LIVING IN THE PRESENCE

LIVING
IN THE
PRESENCE

A Jewish Mindfulness Guide
for Everyday Life

Benjamin Epstein

URIM PUBLICATIONS
Jerusalem • New York

Living in the Presence:
A Jewish Mindfulness Guide for Everyday Life
Benjamin Epstein

Typeset by Ariel Walden

Printed in Israel

First Edition

ISBN 978-1-60280-319-0

Urim Publications
P.O. Box 52287,
Jerusalem 9152102
Israel

www.UrimPublications.com

Library of Congress Cataloging-in-Publication Data in progress.

For

RAZIEL MEIR

HADASSA TIFERET

ADERET EMUNAH

and

SHIMON LEIB

With a love that is eternal

"*Living in the Presence* is a work of art that could only have been written by someone who is truly living in the *present*. My dear friend Dr. Benjy has his finger on the pulse of our turbulent generation, one that is seeking more than ever a practical path of mindfulness and *emunah* to live by. This is a treasure."
   – HaRav Moshe Weinberger, *Marah d'Atra* of Congregation Aish Kodesh, Woodmere, NY and *Mashpia* at Yeshiva University

"Living in the Presence is an invaluable resource for those looking to deepen the connection between mindfulness and spirituality, specifically as it relates to the Jewish faith. While contemporary research makes an effort to remove the transcendent from mindfulness practices, Dr. Epstein deftly articulates that indeed it is the spiritual element that gives mindfulness the ability to transform the totality of how a person relates to his daily existence. This is a book of enormous breadth and depth and will enhance the lives of those who internalize its message."
   – Harold G. Koenig, M.D., Director of the Center for Spirituality, Theology and Health Duke University Medical Center

"Ben Epstein masterfully connects ancient religious wisdom with modern scientific research, providing a roadmap to a more spiritual, happier, existence."
   – Tal Ben-Shahar, Ph.D., Founder of Happiness Studies Academy Co. and Founder of Maytiv Center

"Living in the Presence reveals a way of being that attunes us to the beauty, opportunity and blessing inherent in each moment and every breath. Dr. Epstein is a master craftsman and guide cultivating positivity, confidence, joy, gratitude awareness and self-acceptance. In setting us on the path of spiritual mindfulness, Dr. Benjy's handiwork is an invaluable gift for all of us who yearn for wholeness and deeper connection with others and within. This book serves as a reminder to Dr. Benjy's mantra that "the goal is soul.""
   – Rabbi Judah Mischel, Founder of Tzama Nafshi, Executive Director of Camp Hasc, and *Mashpia* at NCSY

"My religious, spiritual, and professional identities simultaneously intersected while reading *Living in the Presence: A Jewish Mindfulness Guide for Everyday Life*. Dr. Benjamin Epstein has written a unique text that offers sound guidelines for daily mindfulness practice in a busy world. If you are Jewish, if you are a mindfulness practitioner, if you are an acceptance and mindfulness clinician or researcher, or any combination thereof, you should definitely buy and read this book. You will be glad you did!"
   – Amy R. Murrell, Ph.D., Associate Professor of Clinical Psychology at the University of North Texas and Author of the *Becca Epps Series on Bending your Thoughts, Feelings and Behaviors*

Contents

Contents

ᪿ Let everything that hath breath (*neshama*)

praise God. (Psalms 150:6)

ᪿ For each and every breath (*neshima*)

that a person breathes, he needs to praise God.

(*Bereishit Rabbah* 14:9)

Hallelujah

Acknowledgements

This book would not have been possible without the considerable help and support of so many to whom I owe a tremendous debt of gratitude.

First and foremost endless praise and thanks to the "*Echad, Yachid, U'meyuchad- Hayah- Hoveh- V'yihyeh*. Silence is praise to You." (Psalms 65:2)

To the countless individuals who were integral parts of this book becoming a reality, I am deeply grateful for the friendship, time, suggestions, and help you provided to clarify these ideas and for helping me find my voice to express them. In no particular order: Stephanie Tade, Bill Taeusch, Yehudis Golishevsky, George Eltman, Sharon Salzberg, Yael Muskat and the Yeshiva University Counseling Center, Tara Brach, Yaacov David Shulman, Jon Kabat Zinn, Hillel Davis, Susan and Danny Sklarin, Jason Rozen, Menachem Butler, Dovid Bashevkin, Yoel Rosenfeld, Ethan Zanger, Hillel Broder, Rabbi David Aaron, Rav Ari Waxman, Rav Shmuel Braun, Rav Mayer Twersky, Jake, Dan, and Rabbi Nathan Sternhartz.

To Dr. Mitchell L. Schare and the Clinical Psychology program at Hofstra University, I remain eternally grateful for providing me with the skills to transform and heal.

To Tzvi Mauer and his staff at Urim Publications (Pearl Friedman and Shanie Cooper), thank you for your professionalism and skill. Thanks as well to Dan Cohen and his team at Full Court Press.

To the Epstein and Moche families, thank you for all of your love, support, and guidance. Special thanks to my father Gary Epstein who read, and reread the earlier drafts of the book and whose brilliant suggestions helped convey the ideas presented in the most succinct and eloquent way possible. I literally could not have done this without you.

I am connecting myself with this book to all the true *Tzaddikim* that are in our generation, and to all the true *Tzaddikim* resting in dust, especially to our Holy Rabbi, *Tzadik*, *Yesod Olam*, the "Flowing Brook, a Fountain of Wisdom," Rabbi Nachman *ben* Feiga, as well as Rabbi Menachem Mendel Schneerson, and Rav Kalonymus Kalman Shapira, *HYD*. May their merits be a blessing for us all, and may their souls be bound up in the vortex of life.

To my Rebbeim: Rav Avraham Tzvi Kluger, *Shlita* and Rav Moshe Weinberger, *Shlita*. I cannot say that I am worthy to call myself a student of either one of these great men, but this book is my best attempt to convey a fraction of their teachings on these matters. Rav Kluger is a living embodiment of what it means to live in the presence of God and he serves as a model for living with *yishuv hada'at*. Rav Weinberger was and is the inspiration for the ideas presented herein. Rebbe, I hope I have conveyed these ideas accurately, and they are offered to you written in the handwriting of the Rebbe from Vorki and sealed with the kiss of the *Beis Yaakov*. Any errors or lack of clarity should be attributed solely to me, and not, God forbid, their teachings.

To my clients who knowingly or unknowingly helped me formulate these teachings and whose bravery in sharing their personal struggles and triumphs with me never ceases to humble. Thank you for your courage, patience, and willingness to share your journeys with me.

For the past six summers, my family and I have had the opportunity to spend our summers in Camp HASC in Parksville, New York where I work as the Director of Staff Development and Clinical Research. Much of the material that formed this book came from lectures and *sichot* I gave to the staff. Thank you to all the inspiring counselors and staff for providing me the ability to convey these ideas, receive your feedback and for letting me share. Special thanks and love to HASC's Executive Director Rav Judah Mischel (#CROTW) and his wife Ora for giving me the forum and the vote of confidence to share these ideas with the staff and for empowering me to believe in a little bit. Thank you for showing Eleora and me how a person can attach themselves to the *Tzaddik* through the *nekuda* of friendship. Bloodtribe.#

Finally, to my wife and best friend Eleora, thank you for believing in this project from the day I suggested it and even more so for always believing in me. I will never be able to express the gratitude I feel to you for being you and for all that you do for us. "If all of the skies were parchment, and the quills were made of trees, and the ink to write the letters were the water of the seas. . . ."

Introduction

OUR JOURNEY BEGINS with me waiting for a New York City midtown bus. I look up from the book I am reading, and my attention is caught by a bus stop advertisement featuring a picture of the Dalai Lama's serene face and the phrase, "My religion is kindness." I don't return to my book, but just gaze at the message, thinking, "Hey, isn't my religion kindness too?"

For the next few days, I couldn't shake this thought. The Torah teaches, "You must love your neighbor as yourself" (Leviticus 19:18). Rabbi Akiva, one of the preeminent Talmudic scholars, referred to this verse as nothing less than the greatest principle in the Torah. And yet . . . would we think that an ad featuring a person dressed in Hasidic garb or wearing a yarmulke or any other evidently Jewish identity markers, with this verse printed under his smiling face, captures the essence of the Jewish faith? And if not, why not? My religion IS kindness! Where was the disconnect between the pure, distilled essence of Rabbi Akiva's doctrine and contemporary practice?

I realized that I was troubled by the apparent fact that in my self-identification as an observant Jew, and my adherence to a normative set of practices, I had drifted away from the essential, core message offered by my own religion. For a long time, I had considered that I was following the "spiritual path" of Judaism, including its resources of love and kindness. Yet, confronted by the simplicity of the bus kiosk message, I found myself confused and concerned. Somehow, in my pursuit of fulfilling obligations and avoiding the myriad of restrictions, I feared that I had lost sight of the core themes, the unifying principles that are the basis of my religion. I began questioning my aspirations – what was I hoping to gain from the spiritual discipline and religious observance that Judaism prescribed? The candid answer at which I arrived did not resolve my concerns; it exacerbated them.

Essentially, I admitted that I had been conditioned by decades of rigorous Jewish education to view the world as akin to a giant arcade, in which prizes were awarded for certain behavior, practices, and accomplishments. I was diligently searching for the popular arcade game that would provide the most tickets for the least expenditure of skill and effort. It was all about collecting merits or credit that I would ultimately cash in for rewards. I was viewing this world as a mere precursor to the next life. Play by the rules, collect as many tickets as possible, and in the end cash them in for your eternal prize – all the while maintaining an acute subconscious awareness of the corollary: that if you broke the rules, punishment awaited.

Realizing this about myself, I made some discreet inquiries of others and discovered that I was not alone in this attitude. In fact, I became aware that this is a belief system held by many religious Jews, whether consciously or not: maintain a certain lifestyle, follow the rules, and stay out of (too much) trouble until you finally pass Go and collect your prize. If you do it well enough, not only are you assured eternal bliss in the next world, but you can feel pretty good about yourself in this one!

To suggest that this attitude falls considerably short of essential Judaism – and shortchanges its adherent by delivering a deeply deficient version – isn't to deny that Judaism possesses central, immutable tenets that incorporate the concepts of reward and punishment, or are focused on the future, such as belief in the messiah and in an afterlife. The rules exist, they exist for a reason, and they are to be followed. But, there is simply so much more.

Antigonus of Socho, a great Jewish sage, taught "Do not be like a slave who serves the master in order to receive a reward" (*Avot* 1:3). Antigonus was not suggesting of course, that there is no messiah or afterlife. Rather, he uses the fact that there is no explicit mention of either the messiah or an afterlife in the written Torah, to provide a compelling insight: service and reward are necessary, but hardy sufficient. As I delved more deeply, the explanation for the astonishing omission grew clear. These beliefs (as fundamental and imperative as they are) are not meant to be the primary focus of a person on the Jewish spiritual path. They exist. They are among the central precepts of Judaism. But, in themselves, they are peripheral to what Rabbi Akiva understood to be the paradigm.

What then should be a person's focus? What is the purpose of our earthly existence? This book addresses this question and presents an approach culled from the teachings of the great Jewish spiritual masters that span thousands of years.

In short, I hope that on this journey you will discover with me that the purpose of a person's life is to capture and experience some of the benefits of the world-to-come . . . right now, in this world. The supernal bliss that some people spend their entire lives trying to earn in a future life is something that can be attained here.

And there is only one way that a person can attain this: by fully connecting to the present, in whatever form it appears. The present is God's gift to us.

Many spiritual traditions attribute greater or lesser value to living in the present. The Jewish tradition is extraordinary in conjoining the Divine and the mundane, believing at its very core that the present moment holds the key to connecting to the Divine. In Jewish tradition, God is always both transcendent – occupying the throne in the Heavens – and immanent – filling every iota of physical existence.

Psychological research over the past twenty years has demonstrated a variety of benefits that accrue from mindfulness meditation – specifically those meditations that derive from developing skills of how to better live in the present. It should come as no surprise, then, to those of us who believe that Judaism embodies divine wisdom, that only gradually, sometimes over eons, these benefits become apparent to us through the practice of Judaism as well. There appears to be no limit to the potential therapeutic benefits of mindfulness, from alleviating chronic back pain to staving off depressive episodes. Recent research has also begun to demonstrate that an awareness of the transcendent in daily life and a sense of connection to it may produce mental health benefits. These fundamental ideas have been familiar to practitioners of Jewish spirituality for thousands of years.

While most current books on mindfulness focus on alleviating stress and pain (two highly desirable goals), this book aims higher, as befits a book that purports to capture essential Judaism and strives to transform the totality of how a person relates to his daily existence.

This book has an admittedly grand and immodest goal: it aims to alter your mind and change the way you live your life.

The traditional Jewish term for "peace of mind" is *yishuv hada'at* ("settling of the mind"). In cultivating *yishuv hada'at*, we do not aim, like some Eastern religions, to achieve transcendence – i.e. to remove ourselves from whatever predicament, situation, or condition in which we find ourselves. Rather, our goal is to enter fully into whatever is occurring in our lives and meet it with full presence. This *avodah* ("service") is one that requires constant practice and vigilant attention.

In Judaism, the path to achieving peace of mind is not one of strict ascent. Much like the angels on Jacob's ladder, who were in constant flux, a person must both ascend and descend as she treads upon the various rungs of life. The ultimate goal is not to reach a zenith, but to achieve *dveykut* ("connection") and *shleimut* ("wholeness") on every level, as expressed by the verse, "Thou shalt be complete with the Lord thy God" (Deuteronomy 18:13). The voyage itself is the destination.

My realization was that my goal is not merely to amass credits through the performance of good deeds and avoidance of sin, but to attain *shleimut*, which translates to being the most complete version of myself, and not a paradigm of perfection. This gave me the ability to address, and ultimately quell, a gnawing sense of deficiency and inadequacy, a feeling that things were not as I wanted them to be, that something was wrong in my life, that something was missing. Perfection was not attainable; but *shleimut* was within my grasp by actualizing the potential present in myself at each moment, and not merely hoping (and endlessly waiting) for a better future. As I examined my uncomfortable feeling of inadequacy even more deeply, I found that the pain resulting from failure to achieve goals that were beyond human capacity, was emanating from a deep sense of being separate and alone. There were parts of me that I could not accept, and things in my life from which I turned away, again and again. The harshest aspect of that was that I was essentially alone.

While Christianity asserts that such feelings derive from a flawed nature inherited from "original sin," that is not the Jewish approach. Nevertheless, our tradition does acknowledge that something sinister occurred between humanity and divinity in Eden, from which we suffer to this day – something that causes us to feel scattered, separate, and alone. I will return to this idea throughout this book to discuss whether we can identify, address, and rectify that event, and thus attain *shleimut*.

It is universally known that Adam and Eve sinned when they ate from the Tree of Knowledge of Good and Evil. But Judaism teaches that this violation of God's decree was not the primary cause of their fall from grace. Rather, that fall occurred when mankind heeded the blandishments of a deceitful voice suggesting that something external, and not the Divine spark within, could bring happiness and fulfillment. At that moment, alienation and despair were introduced as a part of the human condition, which persists to this day.

Of course, there is nothing inherently evil about seeking resources outside oneself. Rather, the problem lies in the belief that they are the primary sources of happiness and that only through them can one become complete. The moment a person subjugates himself to an external voice that directs him to pursue fulfillment in some externality, he becomes fragmented from his true nature and identity: from his soul. He is constantly looking outward, and thus fleeing from his own divine spark within.

This book is not a mystical work per se. Rather, it aims to be practical and hands-on. But, as part of that goal, it will set forth central tenets of Jewish faith, including mystical ideas – one of which is that each person contains a spark of divinity. When you are in touch with that aspect of yourself, you gain access to clarity and connectedness to that spark. Unencumbered by any baggage from the outside, you are able to clearly hear the voice of your Divine nature emerging from your inner self resources. When the Divine is within, it is superfluous to seek it elsewhere.

A basic purpose of this book is to introduce you to who you are as God made you, and to the gift God has placed within you. If we truly knew, believed, and felt who we were, there would be little room for self-doubt and alienation. Listlessness and existential ennui would disappear in the blink of an eye. But don't take my word for it. Try it. Experience it for yourself – through a series of reflections and practices we will explore together.

When we truly know and accept ourselves, we immediately begin to feel more fulfilled and therefore happier. However, this book aims even higher than helping you connect with your *neshama* ("soul"). It seeks to help you connect with the sparks of Divinity that illuminate every entity and each moment. According to Judaism, the world could not exist without God's constant presence and participation. From this perspective, God is recreating the world at every moment. Our invitation to *dveykut*, to complete connectivity, can only occur in the present moment. The transformative power of the moment derives from the Divinity residing within it. We are not merely connecting to the here and now, but to the Divinity immanent within it and within ourselves.

A person must push aside the veil of self-doubt and alienation. In so doing, he awakens. Then he can see the world as it is – most cogently, he can see God's presence in the world. The prophet Isaiah exhorts us to seek God "where he is to be found," to "call upon him when he is near" (Isaiah 55:6). Surely this is speaking of our present world and not the next.

The Chassidic masters speak of God's presence as being so skillfully hidden that people forget that He is hiding. Poor God, playing hide and seek with people who have stopped searching, who have forgotten that they are even engaged in the game, unaware of the rewards that await the winners. The reward of the Divinity infused in the present moment. This is because the "moment" that we start actually looking, we find Him in plain sight, since He has been present all along. This search requires us to fully inhabit the moment we are in, because it is precisely there and then that He is to be found. And, if we are successful, this book will help you do that – find yourself, and find the God that loves you and animates you.

The Jewish tradition tells of a heavenly voice calling out from Mount Sinai every day: "Return, my children, return!" (*Chagigah* 15a). Every moment is an opportunity to hear this voice, because it is the call of each moment: "Return and return, again and again, to what is, to who you really are."

Be warned. If returning to yourself were easy, there would be no need for this book. Confronting years or decades of misapprehension is challenging. On this journey to wakefulness, there will be obstacles. This book will guide you not to avoid or ignore these, but rather to embrace and accept them. It will present ways to appreciate their utility and their exigency, enabling us to establish a real connection to the here and now, to ourselves and to God, as we use the wisdom of the commandments to anchor us, the teachings of our spiritual masters to guide us, and our own experiences to fortify us. A voyage without obstacles and challenges is a vacation, not a pilgrimage to fulfillment.

Judaism is far from being an ascetic religion. While there are times for contemplation and solitude, restraint and abstinence, the ultimate value of the Torah lies in our fully engaging with and enjoying the physical world and what it has to offer. The Bible is replete with directives to rejoice, be satiated, and experience delight. Most importantly, Judaism endeavors to sanctify time, space, and relationships. The Hebrew word for "holy," *kadosh*, is used in a variety of ways, but its root is about separation and uniqueness. For instance, we usher in the Sabbath by reciting *Kiddush*, get married in a ceremony called *kiddushin*, and recite the prayer of *Kaddish*. By contrast, a *kadesha* is a prostitute, separate and removed from the values and mores that form a constructive society. Separation can sanctify or corrupt; the choice is always ours. The common denominator of all of these usages is that we appoint the present moment, the present space, and the present relationship as separate from and unlike any other that ever was or will be.

The commandments and spiritual teachings of our faith constantly call upon us not to disregard the present moment by getting lost in worries and thoughts about the past and future. Viktor Frankl, the Austrian psychoanalyst who survived the Holocaust, wrote, "In between stimulus and response there is a space, in that space lies our power to choose our response, in our response lies our growth and our freedom." Mankind was given free choice in everything but the ability to reject free choice. In this area, we are always compelled to choose – and these choices are ever-present. This book strives not just to alert you to these present moments of opportunity but to inspire you to uplift and sanctify them by allowing them to be as they are and recognizing their source, knowing them without any veil. That constitutes the ultimate *yichud* ("unification") with the Divine, with the universe, with knowledge, with understanding, with comprehension, with God himself, whose very name, the Tetragrammaton, suggests that the past and future are subsumed in the present. He is, was, and will be.

This book was written for people who want to deepen their appreciation of Judaism and its spiritual practices. It would fall short of its goals if these ideas remained merely theoretical. "Expounding of the law is not the chief thing, but its performance" (*Avot* 1:17). This book provides concise and clear instructions on how to cultivate *yishuv hada'at* in order to attain a life of greater commitment, inspiration, and *dveykut*. Being a better Jew and a happier person are not mutually exclusive; to the contrary, they are mutually interdependent. The focus is on applying these ideas in one's life. From the moment that we wake up to the moment we fall asleep, Judaism's commandments provide us with guidelines that sensitize us to the present. The Hebrew word for "commandment," *mitzvah*, is related to the word *tzavta*, "connecting" or "attachment." The commandments connect us to God in the present moment.

I wrote this book in order to help you gain access to the intimate concepts of *yishuv hada'at* and, more importantly, to implement *yishuv hada'at* in your own life.

Part One (In the Beginning) defines *yishuv hada'at*. This section demonstrates *yishuv hada'at* to be a fundamental requirement for fulfilling the basic tenets of Judaism and for subsequent spiritual growth.

Part Two: *Kavanot* (Intentions) identifies and defines the attitudes and intentions needed to seek and obtain *yishuv hada'at*. It also provides the core philosophical ideas, based upon Judaism's fundamental teachings, regarding the need to be in the here and now.

Part Three: *Avodah* (With Each and Every Breath) provides specific directions on how to incorporate and cultivate *yishuv hada'at* into day-to-day activities.

Part Four: Shabbat: A Day of *Yishuv Hada'at* focuses on the Jewish Day of Mindfulness – Shabbat – as the embodiment of all of these principles, and presents a brief manual on how to connect fully to a complete day of *yishuv hada'at* and mindful practice. As mentioned at the outset, our goal is to achieve in this world, the fulfillment of the world to come. Shabbat is described in Jewish liturgy as "*Me'ein Olam Haba*": a precursor of the world to come. By realizing and embodying the essence of Shabbat, we actualize eternity.

It is my fervent hope that this book will guide those who are seeking to discover or recover the voice that is still calling us from Sinai: "Return, My children, return!"

The constant prayer of our soul is always striving
to emerge from concealment to revelation, to
spread through all the life-powers of our entire
spirit and all the life-powers of our entire body.

This constant prayer is also yearning to reveal
its nature and the might of its action to all of its
surroundings, to the entire world, and to life.

To attain such a level, we must engage in a self-inquiry
that results from our study of Torah and wisdom.

And so the service of learning all of Torah
and all of its wisdom is in itself the constant
revelation of the hidden prayer of our soul.

"The soul of every living thing will bless your name,
Hashem our God."
(*Olat Ra'ayah*)

PART I

In the Beginning

Yishuv Hada'at: Jewish Mindfulness

T HE TERM *YISHUV HADA'AT* appears often in Jewish ethical works, yet is seldom defined. It is commonly understood to mean peace of mind, tranquility, and composure, and often evokes the image of a wise elder proffering sage advice. However, it is possible to understand *yishuv hada'at* on a much deeper level.

The Torah, with its myriad laws and directives, never once explicitly requires a person to be tranquil. As there is no explicit command in the Torah to cultivate *yishuv hada'at*, it is therefore merely viewed as something that, while extremely desirable for its beneficial effects, is not fundamentally required in Judaism. (In fact, the Torah, unlike the Prophets, does not even mention the need to cultivate one's character traits. Moses is said to be modest; Abraham is shown to be generous; we are directed to behave in certain ways to the less fortunate. But there is no set of commandments on character traits. While this omission is dealt with at length by the rabbinic commentaries, few if any would suggest that "peace of mind" takes primacy over any other trait.) But it would be a dreadful error to simply view *yishuv hada'at* as another level to achieve in your progress toward character refinement. This miscalculation begins with the grave error of translating *yishuv hada'at* as mere tranquility or peace of mind. Because in truth, by divining the true meaning and intention of *yishuv hada'at*, one may understand that this character trait is not only desirable but indispensable for one's entire spiritual life.

Anyone who knows me will probably not be at all surprised that this topic, and consequently this book, is something that fascinates me because it is so elusive. Serenity is simply counterintuitive to my nature, and therefore holds an inordinate appeal for me. I tend to get pretty excitable (some might even say over-excitable) and while this ability to be passionate is sometimes a gift, I frequently feel like I let my emotions and thoughts get ahead of me. (Feel free to peruse my teachers' comments from my childhood report cards for further corroboration.) I would often wistfully look at the more even keeled individuals who embodied what I erroneously believed to be *yishuv hada'at* and bemoan the fact that I wasn't born with a more serene, consistent personality. This was usually after I had gotten myself in to some sort of trouble. This regret or in extreme circumstances, shame, would be followed by a resolution to become more reserved or even more withdrawn in an attempt to disengage from life enough to reach a greater level of composure. This commitment usually lasted for a few days, and then I was right back to doing the same thing I had always done. Eventually, I concluded that I wasn't blessed with the persona I so greatly admired, and I resigned myself to accepting my character as it was.

I learned, however, that looking at *yishuv hada'at* in such a binary fashion is actually the source of the problem. If one approaches *yishuv hada'at* as an immutable character trait or temperament that one is either born with or not, a person whose emotions are in a constant state of fluctuation like myself (and the majority of the people I encounter) will inevitably become completely sapped of any resolve to achieve and strive for any modicum of *yishuv hada'at*. As I delved more deeply into the practice and study of *yishuv hada'at*, I discovered that it wasn't merely another character trait for which those who possessed it could be lauded and looked upon with approval, but rather a fundamental necessity for basic human functioning and a critical component of Jewish spiritual practice.

Jewish mysticism teaches that the Hebrew language isn't merely a mode of communication and expression commonly agreed upon as a social convention, but rather should be viewed as the building blocks of the entire cosmos. The Hebrew language is unique in that it not only serves to describe an object but also conveys the essence of what is being transmitted. The word *yishuv* means "settlement" and *da'at* may be translated as "knowledge" or "awareness" – thus, "a settled awareness" which connotes the tranquility most people have come to associate with this term. But at its root the word *da'at* has a more profound meaning.

The mystics explain that the Torah's first usage of a word serves as its archetype in the light of which all of its subsequent usages should be viewed. The first time that *da'at* is used in the Torah is in the verse, "Adam knew his wife, Chava" (Genesis 4:1). Adam knew his wife not merely cognitively but in the most intimate sense. *Da'at* thus indicates fusion, connection, and unification. All other terms used to translate *da'at* are derivations of this original meaning. *The only way to know something is to unite and fully connect with it.*

Thus, *yishuv hada'at* has a much more profound import than "peace of mind." It means "settling into (unifying with) present moment awareness." *Yishuv hada'at* becomes not only the description of a state of mind, but the means to cultivate a state of being. The key to being fully alive and at peace is to be settled in and connected to whatever is happening in one's life, both internally and externally. Peace of mind can only come from a settled mind that is attached to and *knows* not merely cerebrally, but viscerally, whatever is happening here and now. Psychological research has demonstrated that the need to live in the present is as strong as the need to engage in basic physiological functions such as breathing, eating and sleeping. Despite the numerous studies that have demonstrated the deleterious effects on a person's mind and body of regret over the past and anxiety about the future, this point still seems to evade a vast majority of the general populace. In short, if we are constantly living somewhere other than the present, we cannot survive emotionally.

The message of this book is that Judaism takes this concept one critical step forward. Aside from the negative physical and psychological effects of not living in the present, as important as those results are, our primary thesis is that we have a fundamental *spiritual* need to cultivate and develop *yishuv hada'at*, i.e. to achieve unity within the present moment and with present conditions. Even if a person drifts only slightly away from his present reality, he ultimately suffers as severely as a person completely fixated on his past or future. Put simply, they both are not where they are "supposed" to be. Although as opposed to one who is consumed by anxiety or in the grips of a depressive episode, the affected soul might not immediately discern the harmful effects of such minor slippages, as these dissonances accumulate, he inevitably will experience strain and numbness, which can eventually overwhelm him.

What emerges from this is that *yishuv hada'at* isn't limited in its scope – it is not, for instance, "just" a praiseworthy or essential character trait. Rather, it is a fundamental way of being that is indispensable for our most basic spiritual functioning and growth. The misapprehension that *yishuv hada'at* is a state of being that can be attained only by a rare spiritual elite is erroneous and untenable. *Yishuv hada'at* is something that anyone – even a person who feels that he was created with a nervous or anxious (or excitable and overly excitable!) disposition – can achieve. It takes practice, commitment, and dedication, but it is within our reach.

Thus, a person must challenge himself: Can I be less anxious? Can I be happier? Can I cultivate *yishuv hada'at*? And the answer to all of these questions is an unequivocal yes.

In the Beginning:
Choosing Awareness

L ET'S START AT THE VERY BEGINNING. The glorious moment that everything – matter, space, time and life – commenced. For Judaism, this all started at the moment of God's declaration, "Let there be light!" (Genesis 1:3).

Yet from that glorious beginning and all of the magnificent consequences that followed, a simultaneous glaring difficulty arose: the problem of *chillul Hashem* – the "desecration of [the Divine] Name." Within Judaism, this transgression is considered to be *one* of the gravest, if not *the*, gravest of violations. This term is usually understood in either interpersonal terms reflecting on human behavior or in historical terms reflecting on God's behavior. In interpersonal terms, a *chillul Hashem* occurs when a Jew's conduct reflects poorly on himself, on the Jewish people, on the Torah and on God. In historical terms, a *chillul Hashem* occurs when Divine justice seems to be subverted, raising questions of why the righteous suffer and the wicked prosper, and leading people to doubt the existence of an omniscient, omnipotent and all-merciful being.

Unfortunately, if one were asked to determine what event in history constituted the greatest desecration of God's name, there would be no shortage of possible suggestions.

However, the concept of *chillul Hashem* goes much deeper than this, because the literal translation of *chillul* isn't "desecration" but "a void." So this term is more accurately translated as, "a space devoid of [the Divine] Name." That being the case, the single greatest *chillul Hashem* that ever took place was the creation of the world itself, for that one swift gesture brought about the greatest absence of God's presence. In that single moment when God willed the world into existence, there was no greater "desecration" of God's name.

33

How so? The Kabbalah explains that in order for the world to be able to exist God had to "constrict" Himself in order to create a finite world that would not be overwhelmed by the Divine glory. God therefore constricted His presence for the most selfless and loving reasons possible. It is for this reason the verse in Psalms describes our world as a "world built on kindness" (Psalms 89:3). In particular, this gift created a world in which human beings would have free will – a capacity that would enable them to attain ultimate meaning. A newborn child is completely enmeshed with its caregivers, who dote on its every need. You don't need a Ph.D. in psychology to predict the outcome if this reliance and sublimation continues as the child grows up. If the caregiver does not step back and allow for the child to develop on their own, the child's growth will be stilted, with dire long-term consequences. So, very much like a parent, who in the best interest of his child steps back as the child develops, allowing him or her to choose whether to embrace or reject the parent, God also restricted His light, power, and control even as He remained present.

This gift however came at a steep price. In order for God to create a world in which human beings would have free choice, and a possibility of life from which they could derive ultimate meaning, God's presence had to be at least partially withdrawn to avoid overwhelming his finite creations. And in that space that was created, there now stands a void where if man chooses he can reject and even deny the existence of God. Now this is not to suggest that God has "left the building," as some contemporary philosophers have suggested. But God's partial, intentional, and benevolent withdrawal of His presence brought about a void in which a person may not sense Him (in spite of his constant presence) and thus fall prey to the illusion that He is altogether absent. This in itself is the greatest *chillul Hashem*.

The task ahead of us is now clear, even when it is not always apparent. By *choosing* to do so, we affirm the presence of divinity through our mindful intentions and effort. We have the capacity to actualize the presence of God in the world. God challenges us to fill our every moment with the awareness of His presence. Any time we lose this God consciousness, we are in effect causing a *chillul Hashem*. When we are conscious of that, and bring our attention to correct that, our awareness creates a *kiddush Hashem* – a "sanctification of the [Divine] Name." It is our cognizance that the mundane contains divinity that sanctifies the mundane. God is here, but if we do not acknowledge his constant presence, our ability to intersect with the divine withers.

We have been tasked with the responsibility to fill each and every moment with the awareness of God's existence and presence. The moment in which we currently reside is the ever-present litmus test that determines how we will approach this task. Anytime we lose sight of this objective, when our attention drifts and wanders, on some level we are "falling" for the ultimate delusion – the apparent absence of God's presence in the world. Our foremost and most basic obligation to ourselves and to those around us is to reveal God's presence in the world, where at every moment, based on our state of awareness we have the capacity for creating either a *kiddush Hashem* or a *chillul Hashem*. Our awareness of the divinity manifest within the present moment consecrates the present with presence.

Back to Eden: Maintaining Presence

*Y*ISHUV HADA'AT is a state of being that God desires from us at every moment. As noted, it goes beyond the desire to refine one's character and the latest self-help technique. This may come as a surprise to some who may have practiced and practice Judaism completely unaware or devoid of any of these principles. But it is at the core of every one of Judaism's spiritual traditions and practices, including the daily prayers, the prescribed way of dressing, or even while enjoying a meal.

However, although this state is so fundamental that all others depend upon it, it is extremely difficult to cultivate and maintain. Indeed, a person will frequently find it virtually impossible to stay connected to whatever task, thought, or emotion he is engaged in. Often, when I stress the importance of *yishuv hada'at* to my clients they will counter with some form of the following question: "If there is such a fundamental need for the acquisition of this trait, or even more so, if this is the state all others depend upon, why then would this most basic foundational quality be so difficult to cultivate and maintain?"

The answer is that our brains are constantly scanning and judging our internal and external environments – and, related to that, focused on incessantly reviewing the past and worrying about the future.

We do so as an instinctive method of survival, with our "fight or flight" system working remarkably well in times of danger. Unfortunately, when fear-related psychophysiology is activated in a chronic or unwarranted way, it can be detrimental to our health. And that is particularly the case when our judgments are wrong (as they so often tend to be). By indiscriminately believing such

36

judgments – e.g., "This is meaningless," "There is no hope," "I'm no good" – we alienate ourselves even more completely from our surroundings and from ourselves.

The inability to reside in the present moment, along with the concurrent feelings of alienation, began at the time of Creation. The Bible relates that on the third day of Creation God commanded the earth to bring forth "trees of fruit, producing fruit" (Genesis 1:11). The sages explain this to mean that God intended the wood of fruit-bearing trees to possess the same taste as the fruit. However, the earth disobeyed and determined that only the fruit would possess a taste (*Bereishit Rabbah* 5:9). The effects of this seemingly minor act of rebelliousness continue to reverberate to this very day.

God's original intent was that when a person strove to attain a goal he would gain the same pleasure from the means (the "tree") as he would from the goal (the "fruit"). However, because of the earth's miscalculation we do not automatically experience the joy of accomplishment in every step of any process we undertake. The desire to reach the fruit often consumes us to such a degree that we are unable to derive pleasure and meaning from the process that is fundamental to its attainment. Ironically, after a person achieves a goal, he may be left feeling as empty as before, seduced initially by the thought that once he got "there," he would be happy. But when he reaches the goal, he realizes that there is no "there," because he lacks the skill of being happy. That is to say, he lacks the fundamentals of *yishuv hada'at*, which can be provided by no external object.

Adam was guilty of the same sin as the earth when he separated the fruit from the tree. That too is an expression of differentiating between the journey and the destination, the means and the end, the process and the zenith. And every time we do that – every time we focus on the goal and not on the process – we re-enact that original sin and deviate from the path that God intended for us.

Because Adam removed the fruit from the tree, God cursed him with death. It was not a physical death, as evidenced by the fact that he did not die. Nor was his sentence mitigated; rather, death was indeed introduced into the world the second the fruit was no longer connected to the tree. The moment an individual believes he can only feel joy at the final goal, he may no longer be called "living." We are still suffering from that curse – from a death that can occur even as we physically remain alive. This curse casts a veil over our eyes, preventing us from seeing the sublime and eternal life contained in every moment. If a person accepts this illusion, if he believes that he can only feel joy when he reaches a goal, he can no longer be said to be truly alive. Rather, he is lost in a world of imagination, bolstered by idealized memories of the past and focusing on ethereal hopes for tomorrow, even as internally he is eroding.

But if a person can keep the fruit connected to the tree, he experiences life and *yishuv hada'at*. He repairs the original sin and achieves the true goal of Jewish spirituality: the taste of the world to come in this world.

Birth and Rebirth: Divinity Within

I ONCE SAW A COMMERCIAL that showed a father and his young daughter sitting in a field, watching the sun setting over the mountains. As the sun dipped towards invisibility, the father whispered to his daughter, "Going . . . going . . . gone." And when it disappeared, she turned to him and said, "Do it again, Daddy."

A few years later, this memory was in my thoughts when I took my four-year-old daughter onto the balcony of a twelfth floor apartment facing the Mediterranean Sea as the sun was setting. Now I anticipated my own "Do it again, Daddy" moment; something that she would remember and tell her own children about. Much to my chagrin, as the sun sank below the horizon, she turned to me and asked, "Why don't trees grow up to the sky?" I was shocked. Disappointed. That's it? That's all I'm going to get? Still, I held onto my belief that this could be a transformative moment in her life.

"Did you just see that?" I asked her. "Wasn't it beautiful?"

"Yes," she answered, "but how come they don't just keep growing?" And then she went inside to ask her mother.

I was left deflated, wondering where I had gone wrong.

The sunset was as magnificent as it had always been, so clearly the fault lay elsewhere – and that was in my expectation of what I had wanted to transpire. I had superimposed my own expectations on the moment and was thus unable to appreciate and relish the wonder of the question that was actually illuminating the moment.

We rarely experience things as they are. Everything that we see and feel is colored by our thoughts, memories, beliefs and expectations. I was so set on having the type of experience I had imagined and anticipated that I couldn't appreciate the wonder and uniqueness of the reality that actually was (which, in retrospect, was pretty good).

We are always expecting, when we could be accepting. The way to get past this barrier is to cultivate the *kavanah* (intention) of *chiddush*. *Chiddush* – which comes from the root word *chadash*, "new" – means innovation or revelation. The practice of *chiddush* is the cultivation of an ability to see things without preconceived interpretations: to know that one does *not know* and to appreciate what is, rather than what might be. This *kavanah* can be both humbling and liberating. It is humbling in that we admit that we rarely know exactly what things are, even if we are looking right at them; and it is liberating in that we may begin to see things as they *truly* are.

How often have our first impressions about someone or something been wrong? I am sure we can all recall a time when we thought that someone had behaved rudely towards us, only to find out they had just lost a loved one, or when someone we felt was ignoring us simply didn't see us. Cultivating your ability to approach each situation with a perspective of *chiddush* can minimize these misinterpretations and even eliminate them. When the sages taught us that the wise man is one who is able to learn from all men, they were most certainly not referring to the person who finished at the top of his class at Harvard.

In many meditative traditions, the cultivation of this mindset is critically important to attaining greater consciousness and compassion. For the Jewish spiritual seeker, this mindset forms the basis of cultivating *yishuv hada'at*.

God's creation of this world out of absolute nothingness required an act unlike anything we can imagine. In particular, it required divinity to imbue itself into the creative process. God's ten utterances of creation (e.g., "Let there be light," "Let there be a firmament") constituted the building blocks of creation. They served not only as a directive but also as the reality that they articulated. When God first pronounced these words, they became clothed in the universe as a direct infusion from God into our reality. An aspect of the infinite became imbued in the finite.

These sustaining utterances continue to generate the universe at every moment. In their Divine nature, they are filled with vitality and are themselves enduring. Everything is made vital and sustained through these utterances and their permutations. The letters of God's speech are clothed in every aspect of creation.

The Psalmist alludes to this when he says, "Your word stands in the heavens forever" (Psalms 119:89). These words and letters are perpetually receiving a current of energy from their Divine source and transforming it into existence.

The sky that we look at, the table in front of us – all of reality as we know it – is a function of these words. Every aspect of this world is dependent at every second on this invigorating life force and energy coming at every moment from God.

If these letters would be retracted for even a moment, if for one second the letters winked out of existence, everything would cease to be just as before the world existed. It wouldn't merely falter, it would disintegrate into the nothingness that prevailed before those words were uttered. This rule applies not only in the physical world, but extends from the most spiritual of realms to the smallest particle. If for the smallest fragment of time the letters of existence were to cease, then all would cease to be.

When we look at the world around us, when we look at the people we love, and when we look at ourselves, we are looking at an existence that is being recreated every instant and every moment. The words God said weren't merely for us to know what was done in the past because it's not a matter of knowing. It's a matter of being. It's what is happening this very moment. And the next and the next. This constant state of creation can animate us with the wonder and desire to marvel in and perpetually enjoy God's handiwork.

When God said those words, "exhaled" those words, the words whose letters derived from the "*kishkes*" of existence (the innermost being of existence), the words not only became clothed in the firmament and earth. They formed a direct connection and infusion from God with reality as we know it. Our existence depends on the perpetual sustenance of this connection, because that connection is what infuses and invigorates life as we know it. An aspect of the infinite becomes clothed in the finite. The letters of God's words became garbed in, and animate, reality. All of creation is nothing more than the heart in which God himself is attired. The reality that constantly surrounds us is God Himself.

Internalized properly, this can be a radical and refreshing realization. By fully attaching yourself to the idea that everything is infused with divinity, everything in your life becomes enlivened. Everything does truly become illuminated with the presence of God. And what is transpiring in that very moment is the ultimate means of forming a connection with the Divine.

The Missing Piece:
Two Sides of the Same Coin

O NE OF MY FAVORITE BOOKS from childhood is a book titled *The Missing Piece*. In it, the author, Shel Silverstein, brilliantly describes an almost whole circle that seeks a "missing piece" to complete it. The author brilliantly depicts a Pacman-esque figure searching for love and purpose. Known primarily as a children's book, it is filled with many profound morals and lessons for life. The story can be described as a commentary on how, more often than not, we don't know what is best for us, and on the futility of searching for the ideal anything. But I think the simplest (and probably most important) message of this childhood classic is that the search for completion is often flawed. The demand to be always searching, looking, seeking for something "other" to complete us is fundamentally flawed. That is because things, even when they are "incomplete," are also perfect in their own way. But while perfection is not something that can ever be completely reached, there is a possibility of achieving wholeness for all of our missing pieces.

> Make thee two trumpets of silver; of beaten work shalt thou make them; and they shall be unto thee for the calling of the congregation, and for causing the camps to set forward.
>
> Numbers 10:2

The creation and blowing of silver trumpets, for the calling of the camp as well as for causing the camps to move forward, is the physical manifestation of a divine truth that resonates deeply in our daily lives. In Jewish spiritual literature, everything that exists in the world contains two components. The components are the physical matter, which is referred to as *chomer*, and the spiritual element, which is referred to as the object's *tzurah*. Everything exists with a form and its spirit. The Hebrew word for trumpet, *chatzotrot*, is an amalgam of the words *chatzi*, which means "half," and *tzurah*, which refers to this spiritual reality. This command is a perpetual call to this existential truth. Everything we experience is only half. We are all missing pieces.

The great Maggid of Mezeritch and his students teach that God too is missing a piece. This is obviously a pretty radical statement, because believing oneself to be deficient and requiring God to fill that void is one thing. To say that the converse is also true borders on heresy. And yet God, perfect in His essence, has created a reality that He too, in a manner of speaking, is deficient without His people. God is manifest as one half of the coin, while the Jewish people are the other half, and only when these two are joined together do we have the formation of these two silver trumpets in their complete form.

There is an ever-present, deep longing for this union to occur. The silver material that the trumpets were formed from is *kesef* in Hebrew, related to the word *kisufin*, "longing." (This idea is expressed in the verse from Psalms 84:2, "My soul yearneth, yea, even pineth for the courts of the Lord.") Each party longs to fill the void of the other. The deeper meaning of the two trumpets of silver, the *chatzotrot kesef*, is the revelation of a world of incomplete forms that are in a state of unceasing longing. God is filled with longing for His other half, the Jewish people, while the Jewish people are also filled with a great yearning and desire to have their void filled with God's presence. Each can only be whole when fused with the other.

While this is very beautiful, the question now becomes, what do trumpets have to do with this profound idea? The blowing of the trumpets somehow illustrates two incomplete halves yearning to be joined to complete one another.

> He [the son of Azzai] used to say: Do not be disrespectful of
> any person and do not be dismissive of anything, for there is
> no person who does not have his hour, and there is no thing
> which does not have its place. (*Avot* 4:3)

The trumpets were used primarily on four specific occasions. In the desert, they were used to gather the people together, as well as to inform them that it was time to move. Additionally, they were also blown at times of war and during the festivals. The *Sefer Yetzirah*, perhaps one of the most ancient works of Kabbalah, explains that just as everything that we experience in the world is three-dimensional, everything exists on three levels. These three building blocks of reality are space, time and soul. In Hebrew this is known as *olam*, *shanah* and *nefesh* (literally, world, year and soul).

"There is nothing that does not have a place." Everything exists in a particular dimension of space. This is the dimension of *olam*, "space."

"Everything has its time." "A time to love and a time to hate, a time for war and a time for peace" (Ecclesiastes 3:8). Everything has its moment. This is the dimension of *shanah*, "time."

"Do not be disrespectful of any person." In spite of our differences, every person has his or her own unique contribution to make. This is the dimension of *nefesh*, "soul." And every *nefesh* has its place and time. And every time has its *nefesh* and place as well.

When the trumpets, the symbols of the half form, were blown to gather the people, the call was a reminder that no person is complete on his own. There is another half that he needs to complete. There are certain spiritual practices that only a select few can do. Some practices are prescribed only for men, and some only for women. Others are mandated for the priests and some are only for the king. But by recognizing that I am only half, and by connecting to others, I am completing that half form. In the realm of physical bodies, we are distinct, separate entities.

Separation comes from identifying solely with the incomplete, broken pieces of the physical world. But when a person connects on the level of the soul, with the recognition that he is only half without the other, then he can transcend the separation. A person can erroneously believe himself to be completely self-sufficient, but it doesn't change the reality that we are all only half. The blowing of the trumpets to bring people together is the fusion and joining of two forms. In order to be complete, I must remember that I am both whole and part of a whole. This does not contradict the fact that each part is indispensable and whole with reference to itself. But in this dialectical model, to complete myself, I must be joined with others. This is a reminder in the dimension of soul.

The trumpets were blown to signal the movement of the camps.

A person's place is constantly changing. This doesn't mean that in order to experience this a person has to get out and become a world traveler. We are always meeting up with new places: new routes to get to work, the sudden business trip, or the emergency visit to the hospital. The world is in constant motion. Each experience is an opportunity to actualize our existence, to manifest our Godly characteristics. And each place we encounter, no matter how mundane it may seem, is also calling out to us to complete it, to fill the void that was left until precisely the moment we arrived, a reminder in the dimension of space.

The trumpets were blown during times of war and, at times of peace, for the festivals. Joyous times and sad times – we are perpetually encountering new times. There has never been a repeated moment in our lives. Every moment is different. Every moment is a calling that is asking to be filled, a reminder in the dimension of time.

People we think we know, places we are intimately familiar with, times that seem to be indistinguishable from one another – never once has there been a person or a place or a time that's been repeated. The river of life is constantly flowing, and we can never reenter it at the same place. We are perpetually meeting new times, arriving at new places, encountering new people. This present moment never was nor will it ever be again. Reality is always changing constantly along these three levels of place, time and soul.

There are places in a person's life to which he feels more spirituality connected, places that may be considered unique for him. In those places, he feels that he is able to connect on a deeper level. Conversely, there are places in which a person feels that there is not a speck of Divinity to be found, places that leave him feeling empty and frigid from their lack of warmth and spirit. Likewise, there are certain times, similar to certain places, when a person feels this preternatural connection and energy. And, there are, inevitably, times that are difficult, bereft of any inspiration or joy. Similarly, there are people we encounter who inspire and stimulate growth, and others we recoil from or who pull us away from our relationship with God and our values. To paraphrase one of the slogans from Alcoholics Anonymous, "people, places and things, they all have an effect on us." Certain times, places and people draw us closer to Divinity, closer to the valued direction of our lives, whereas we feel that certain times, places and people obstruct us from this path. But that does not, cannot, mean that all of them are not infused with the divine spark, waiting only to be uncovered and discovered.

I held him, and would not let him go.   *Song of Songs* 3:4

The nature of a person who is not living with *yishuv hada'at*, who is not conscious that this moment is an encounter with Divinity, can be deluded into thinking there are particular places that are "worthy" and "good" places which feel illuminated, places where a person may proclaim "here and only here can I adequately serve God!" In contrast, there are other places that don't inspire the same devotion and spiritual fervor, places that don't trigger any sense of religious feeling. These places are deemed not appropriate, and even devoid of God.

Likewise, there can be certain times in life when a feeling of exaltedness takes over. A person can tell himself that now is a time for service. This feels like an opportune time for me to open my mouth in praise! Now I can find it in my heart to approach and be closer to my Creator. Other times, the converse of this may also be true. Times where a person feels disinterested, times when the heart feels closed, the feeling that right now is just not the right time. Our minds are quick to justify our apathy and disinterest. Some form of this conversation has played out in my head on more occasions than I care to admit. "What else could You expect from me? If only I were in *that* place. If only it were happening during *another* time. But I am not there today. It's not now, and maybe it will be at some point, but it is certainly not now." Or some variation of this thought process.

A person can go through his entire life with a mantra of "tomorrow and tomorrow and tomorrow." "Perhaps in a different time or, better yet, in another place. This wouldn't really be a challenge if I had been brought up in different surroundings. Then I would be able to [insert lofty accomplishment here]. But right now? Right here? With these people? My hands are simply tied."

This is the message of the trumpets, the message of the half-form: Every person. Every time. Every place. When you arrive, all that exists is half. From time immemorial, this place, this time, this person has been broken, waiting for you to fill the void. This doesn't mean that you need to have a meaningful, romantic relationship with the person you just met sitting next to you on the bus. But there is something you can do to complete that person, whatever that may be. And there is something with which that moment can fill *you* with as well. This missing piece is waiting to be filled precisely in that place left partially complete that only you can fill in yourself, in order to form a complete union. Each encounter is filled with the question of, "What does this moment, place or person I am with demand of me right now?"

These trumpets are blown whenever a person moves from place to place, to remind him that not only "wherever you go, there you are," but "there you are needed, and there He is waiting for you."

You live with the ever-present awareness that wherever you go God brought you there. And is there waiting for you. When you are in that place and in that time, you are filled with the knowledge and belief that this place is only a half, waiting for you, and you are only a half, waiting for this place. You have a longing to complete and be completed, to fix and uplift this place that you are in, and not any other. You have the empowering understanding that there is no one else who can do this, by being who I am and doing what I am able to do, wherever you are, in specifically that place and time. That is what is always being asked of you, no matter where or when. *There is no thing which does not have its place.* "Fill me. Complete me." Complete yourself.

Time. Every single moment is a broken piece of time in which God has placed you in so that you may fix it with the resources you have at hand at precisely that time. Every moment that you see is half of a moment. Your response completes the moment, in that moment in your life and not in any other, nor can it be accomplished by any other person. The debilitating states of mind that paralyze us with the notion that "it would be better if someone else did it" or "perhaps at a different time" may be replaced with the awareness, *"for there is no person who does not have his hour."* And this hour is right now. Every moment you see is waiting to be filled with your half. Every moment is replete with opportunity and challenge.

The trumpets were blown at times of gathering. Every single person you encounter – your family, your spouse, your friends, your casual acquaintances, your peers – is waiting to be completed by you. Gather everyone together. Remember that you are only half.

And you are needed as much as you need others. Whether you meet a person for the first time or for the thousandth time, remember, like the piercing sound of a trumpet blast: this is a person waiting for you. It could be a simple hello, a gesture, a nod, or a shoulder to cry on. It might be saying goodbye. But there is always the awareness that this is a half waiting for another half. It's not just a life-altering interaction, although it might be that too. Do not be disrespectful of any person and do not be dismissive of anything, for right now, in this moment, in this place, there is a soul that's only half.

This is the antidote to the profound sense of alienation that we often feel between ourselves and the people around us, the surroundings in which we find ourselves, and the times in our lives. But there is an even more profound division that takes place internally. The profound division that occurs between a person's divine soul and physical body is the paradigm of these two halves longing to be completed. There is a part of a person that craves spirituality, his divine spirit, whereas there is another part that is interested primarily in the needs and desires of physical existence. Man himself is the paradigm of these two shattered forms. The soul always yearns for that which is higher, while the body is encumbered by the heaviness of physicality.

But here too is the possibility for the ultimate unification, where soul meets body to join the two and complete the circle. When you are living completely in the moment, you are unfragmented. Living with the full awareness and consciousness of your Divinity and the Divinity that surrounds you fuses something from this world below with the world above. This broken piece of heaven has been longing for earth, and this broken piece of earth has been longing for heaven. You take these two pieces and forge them into a complete circle. If you eat after first reciting a blessing, mindful of the food you are putting in your mouth and grateful for the sustenance it provides, that's *yishuv hada'at*. There are no magic or complex spiritual devotions. *Yishuv hada'at* is a simple, profound recognition of the here and now, awareness of the amazing union that is occurring. Two separate forces join together to become whole.

This is Jewish mindfulness. This is living with the secret of creation, living with the feeling, the felt sense, that this half-ness does not connote deficiency. Rather, this half-ness was created to fill and be filled, with one's ever-present recognition that his Godly soul is the other half. Every single moment, person and place you encounter, or happen to be with, or find yourself in, is a half form that is silver (*kesef*), begging for completion, longing for completion. And in the same way that connectivity can occur with my peers, with the places in which I find myself and the times in which I am living, I can fully connect to myself at any moment and achieve the ultimate unification. Completion. Today.

Wisdom and Understanding

THE INTRODUCTION to the *Tikunei Zohar* associates the meaning of Creation and the cosmos with the *dagesh* (a diacritic mark in the Hebrew language represented by a dot within the letter) in the first letter of the Torah, *bet*. "What is the beginning? The inner dot, regarding which the verse states: 'All of the riches of the king's daughter are within' (Psalms 45:13)." This means that within each and every one of us resides this one point, this one central axis around which our inner world revolves.

To understand this "point" is to understand everything. So we return to where everything starts in order to understand the forces that lie at the root of all creation, because each and every one of us is created in the exact same fashion that the world was created. And just as the world is recreated on a constant basis, each and every one of us is recreated moment by moment. To understand the beginning is to understand the world around us and ourselves.

> The Lord by wisdom founded the earth; by understanding He established the heavens.   (Proverbs 3:19)

The world we inhabit was created with wisdom and understanding. These two elemental forces infuse creation and its creatures with the life force of creation and the Creator.

What are these forces of wisdom and understanding, and how do they apply to me? Where can they be found? How can they be accessed and cultivated? And what is my relationship to these building blocks of creation?

These energies are found everywhere and in everything – a spiritual periodic table if you will. They are not merely concepts, theories, personality traits or styles. They cannot be made into simple topographies, where you can say, "I am this type and not that type." They are mindsets that determine the reality around us. Wisdom (*chochmah*) and understanding (*binah*) can be either the catalyst for all of our growth and development or the root of our suffering and anguish, as well.

A parable: A weary traveler is walking through a dark forest fretting, his last candle about to expire. Alone and afraid, paralyzed with fear, barely able to even take another step, he cannot see the road ahead, nor is he sure of which direction to follow. Suddenly a great crack of lightning flashes from the sky. And for that split second everything is clear: where the road is leading and what direction to travel. Everything is illuminated.

That flash, that instant of clarity, that ability to see the "big picture," the whole picture – that is *chochmah*. We have all experienced this at some point in our lives. It is the ability to look at anything, anyone, any place, even ourselves, and see the fullness and potential of all that might be. The potential, with all of the energy and power of any possible outcome, is contained in this moment. It is all right here, right now. In that moment, you are living in the experience of the actual idea, which includes the entirety of all that can potentially develop. It is the "first freedom" latent with a multitude of choices arrayed before us.

But that strength (in Hebrew, *ko'ach*) is still in a state of "What is it?" (in Hebrew, *mah*). The unlimited potential remains abstract.

Therefore, there is a second phase, the offspring of that seed of *chochmah*, which brings *chochmah* to fruition. Wisdom requires understanding to be actualized. *Binah* is understanding; it is the transformation of the idea into something real: stage after stage, step by step, with critical thinking, dissection and analysis. It is the inevitable descent into the details. It is where we abandon some of the limitless possibilities of *chochmah* to focus on just a few of them. It is the progress into the world of doing and details. The entirety of the life of the mind can be said to be comprised of these two "stations."

The nature of *chochmah* is the ability to perceive the wholeness and interconnectedness of everything. It literally contains all. It is akin to the ability of sight, with its capability to see something in its entirety. There are countless components included in any vista, but the eye can contain it all in one sweeping glance. This is the personification of *chochmah* – the ability to absorb the entire wonder of creation in one unified image. But any attempt to communicate that unified picture to another will result in fragmentation. The words dissect the holistic experience into details and parts, none of which captures the full reality. The nature of *binah* is that of separating, individuating, categorizing and classifying, so that the entirety can be comprehended and mastered. While I am unable to hear two people at once, I am able to see hundreds in a single glance. This division and separation of components allows for the abstract to become palpable.

Everything we do is determined and influenced by the balance of *chochmah* and *binah*. They are referred to in the Kabbalistic literature as two friends who should never be separated. And in truth they never really have to be, because when utilized correctly *binah* is simply the outgrowth of *chochmah*, the concurrent stage where every single detail is able to be illuminated with the light of that original spark. As a consequence, even while a person is in a state of *binah*, every single detail can contain the wholeness of the big picture. When applied correctly, the synergy becomes a fluid, organic whole.

But as is often the case, without careful attention, this delicate balance is tenuously maintained. The planning stages of every endeavor become fraught with pitfalls. And that is all the more so when the actual "doing" begins. In the *binah* state, it becomes very easy to be disconnected entirely from *chochmah*. Our choices become rigid and often myopic, based simply on avoiding disappointment or seeking instant gratification. We lose sight of the whole picture, because we are engrossed in mastering a detail. And without constant reminders and practice, a person often gets "lost" in the details – or worse, becomes dejected when the details inevitably become too overwhelming.

The frustration and difficulties of life can often be summed up by the separation between *chochmah* and *binah*. This division can play itself out in so many different forms and facets of life. But the depth of the matter remains the same: the actual self vs. the idealized self, the process of always becoming while never being. The question that life constantly asks of us is, "Can I simultaneously shine the light of connectedness and wholeness into the individuality and separateness of day-to-day existence?" In other words, can we apply this dialectic to ourselves as being both whole and separate at the same time? The purpose is for everything to come together, for each detail to be filled with the light of the whole picture. Shabbat is a perfect example of living with the light of *chochmah*. And we are tasked to take that light and infuse the six days of the week, the world of *binah*, with it. And it is all a matter of awareness and perception. There is no structural impediment to unifying the two, if we have the will to do it. This is the bringing of the Sabbath into the six days of the week. It is the *point* of everything.

The world is moving away from *chochmah* at an alarming pace. We are hyper-focused on building and earning, without ever stopping to simply ask why. What a great misfortune for a person who remains stuck *solely* in a *binah* mindset without ever incorporating *chochmah*. It is having access to individual tasks but not the entire design, not the blueprint. But isn't this how we often go through life? Feeling as though there are lots of details that we need to take care of but without any light with which to invigorate and enliven them. Take a typical mundane day. How do I look at routine when I am changing a diaper or taking out the trash or doing the dishes? If these moments are not connected to the bigger picture of who this child is and what it means to be a parent, a spouse, a sibling, a friend – then these details can become very tiring and mindless and sometimes even painful.

For those traveling the spiritual path, there are lots of laws to follow, but oftentimes these laws are totally bereft of God. When prayer ceases to be a dialogue with a caring God, when our tasks lack personal connection and an overarching sense of wholeness – that is a life of *binah* without *chochmah*. It becomes a life dimmed and overburdened by the chasm created by this separation.

The person living with the *binah* mode simultaneously infused with the mindset of *chochmah* is able to take any situation he or she is in and seek out the inner point, the core of the matter. He or she will not get bogged down with details, but rather see the root of the situation without getting snagged in the branches of particulars. He can sense the essence, because when looking with *chochmah* he always sees the big picture. He might instead acknowledge that at this moment he is unable to do just that, but that he knows that the big picture is there. The mind becomes expansive, able to contain the multitudes of life without becoming hyper-fixated on any one single detail, feeling or thought, to – quite simply – get to the heart of the matter. Understand: without *binah*, one accomplishes nothing, a visionary without a methodology. But without *chochmah*, one's life amounts to nothing except a surfeit of meaningless detail.

This dichotomy of *chochmah* without *binah* and vice versa occurs at work, in friendships, in the most intimate relationships, and, most importantly, in relationship with oneself. The mode of *chochmah* is the ability to understand the quality of something without getting carried away with superficialities, such as "how many" or "how expensive" or any other external trapping. In the world of *chochmah*, there is no significance to quantity without quality. Numbers aren't the endgame. By not getting sidetracked with the details that inevitably surface, one is able to see how there is a perpetual underlying and unifying current that runs through creation. Everything is in the first dot of *Bereishit* ("In the beginning").

"Who is wise? One who learns from every one" (*Avot* 4:1). For the person in *chochmah* mode, there are no preconditions in order to learn something and receive something new. No matter where he is, he can attach himself to the education available in the ambient environment. This practice is the ability to receive something and integrate it into his own world without getting lost in how that idea may be presented. There is always a lesson to be learned. So the present must never be wasted.

"Who is wise? He who recognizes his place" (ibid.). For the person in *chochmah* mode, his place is exactly where he is. He doesn't require any specific environment, and he doesn't set any preconditions. He is able to thrive anywhere. He knows his place, because his place is right here, wherever he happens to be. Differences and change do not overwhelm him.

From the *binah* perspective, there is a propensity to get very disoriented if the details aren't just so. Conditions must not only be good but must be exactly appropriate to his needs. Even the slightest variation or turbulence can throw him off course.

"Who is wise? He who is able to discern the consequences of his actions" (ibid.). But he must do more than just be able to discern consequences, because the Hebrew word for "consequences" (*nolad*, literally, "born") refers to that which is being initiated right now from whatever is transpiring. He is able to see the present as something that subsumes all that will eventuate, to perceive the kernel of truth and meaning in whatever is. And it is being born right now, at this very moment; all he needs is be able to discern it.

One tends to become frustrated when one resides in the *binah* mode for too long, as the details inescapably begin to slowly wear him/her down. The *binah* mode always wants to see how things are changing or to make change happen faster. Naturally, if things aren't happening at the pace we want them to, we get discouraged, ultimately abandoning crucial personal journeys before they even begin. Imagine how many lofty, genuine, spiritual treks have ended due to these frustrations. How many goals have been abandoned? How many desires left to expire? We lose our focus and our conviction because we have forgotten to bear in mind the *chochmah* inherent in what we are doing.

When we are consumed with just getting things done, the *chochmah* can fly right out the window. When we are feeling anxious or depressed or just feeling stuck in the general malaise of life, then the light of *chochmah* can become easily extinguished. For *binah*, everything has to be just right. For *chochmah*, everything just has to be. *Binah* can then direct one's untapped potential into the seeming minutia and details of life, bringing about a perfect symbiosis.

When a person is living a life that is primarily guided by, and living with, this attribute of *chochmah*, he must eventually come to the practical. However the "main thing," the "big picture," always remains in the forefront of his mind. Even the fact that this *chochmah* may move from potential to actual, from vision to reality, eventually coming into fruition is secondary. The critical goal is the ability to "keep the main thing as the main thing." It is the wisdom to know the difference between accepting what I cannot change and having the courage to change the things I can.

For those of us who are living firmly planted in just the *binah* mode, your mind is probably screaming, "How then will I gauge my accomplishments? How will I measure success and failure?" I require specific, discrete tasks so that I can keep score. These questions and frustrations, which arise in one form or another, are all asking the same thing. "Who am I if I am not what I am doing?"

These questions do not trouble the person living in the *chochmah* mode. His value is not based on these arbitrary markers. The *chochmah* mindset permits the individual to have values that are not merely quantitative. They are very often difficult to discern and describe. Can peace of mind be measured by amount? Is it something you can take a picture of? Can connectivity or grace be calculated? Can feeling whole be quantified?

The force of *binah* compels a person to go into the future with pre-made plans and expectations, with drawings and plans (but not, remember, the blueprint). The force of *chochmah* does not operate with a specific plan for the future, because it is deeply rooted in the present. Of course, there is always a path and a trajectory, and nothing can sway him from it. But that is not where the focus or preoccupations reside. Negative thoughts and emotions and even painful experiences serve only as fleeting diversions. The way of *chochmah* is simply for the light of this – and only this – moment to fill the person completely. The path forward will reveal itself once the ultimate objective is clear.

Moving from *binah* to *chochmah* requires a shift of paradigm and attention. The questions that typically abound in a person's mind about what benefits he is deriving dissipate with the recognition that they are coming from a *binah* mindset. Don't misunderstand. This is not an antinomian approach allowing a person to neglect his service and responsibilities. The details are essential. Vision alone is too insubstantial to be meaningful. Rather, one whose life is infused with *chochmah* no longer needs a token economy to gauge his success and failures. Whereas my child needs a sticker chart to motivate her to stay in her bed at night, and that works fairly well, it would be funny – and more likely disturbing – if she were still to need this at the age of thirty. The *binah* mindset is essential for the necessary framework to be created and for a person to realize the vision. But is that our end game? Every step brings a person closer to his valued direction in life – not because of anything it will necessarily accomplish but because of what he/she is doing right now. If our actions become just a means for simply moving to the next step or some sort of metric to gauge success, then life can quickly grow overwhelming. But if we connect to the spark that infuses everything, then that moment is perfect just the way it is right now. As long as our deeds are in the context of *chochmah*, they retain meaning. When they themselves become the goal, they are empty.

This shift occurs when a person wants to expand beyond the self to no-self (know self): to a realm where every moment is a new opportunity for an encounter, every word is a new revelation, and every breath is new life. Nothing is more liberating than a person who is freed from the confinement of personal selfishness and selfness to seek the holiness of faith and Torah by connecting to the One who has given us this faith.

Binah can take over and run away with a person's Judaism and beliefs while leaving his *chochmah* in the dust. In many ways, a life of *binah*, although more physically demanding, can be far easier than the mental demands of *chochmah*, which require of a person the demanding work of discovering who he is and before whom he is standing. "Do this" and "Don't do that" (*binah*) is a much easier way of living than "Be this" and "Don't be that" (*chochmah*). The details of *halacha* (Jewish law) are components in a life of the soul, but they only become truly meaningful when they engage the heart in the mode of being, of always being the person he aspires to become (*chochmah*).

When a person has cultivated and refined this *chochmah* mindset, he is able to descend into the world of *binah*, all the while shining the light of *chochmah* on each of the details. He is able to connect to the infinite mind of the Creator and the Divine blueprint that is contained in every moment.

Being and Becoming:
Where Are We Going?

THERE ARE BASICALLY TWO STAGES to every journey. First, a person has to know where he is headed; and second, he has to have plans to get there. Once a person has set out with a certain end point or goal in mind, he needs to establish some sort of direction (in Hebrew, *kivun*) in order to achieve his objective or arrive at his destination.

So at the beginning of any journey a person must clearly define the goal of the undertaking – known in the Hebrew vernacular as the *tachlit*. Once the *tachlit* has been established, then planning how to achieve this *tachlit* begins. (As with *chochmah* and *binah* – you require both.)

So where are we going? And how are we getting there? Thousands of years ago, our forefather Abraham answered God's command, *Lech lecha-* "Go (from) yourself" (Genesis 12:1). That same exact directive propels and drives us towards our goals as well. Much has been written about Abraham's response to this Divine call – how Abraham was unique not in that he listened to what God asked him to do (I think most of us would pack our bags without hesitation if God tapped us on the shoulder and told us it was time for a geographical relocation), but that he heard God at all. The directive of *lech lecha* was stated by God for everyone in the world to hear, and it is an uninterrupted directive to all of Abraham's children. Abraham differed from the world in that he not only heard the call but he heeded it as well.

Anyone on the Jewish spiritual path is marching to the call that our forefather Abraham internalized thousands of years ago: *Lech lecha*. This call was not merely a command to leave his father's house and homeland but to go inward. "Go to yourself. Discover who you really are, because only then will you be able to discover who I really am," says God.

So we trek onward with *lech lecha* shining in our hearts and minds. These words give us the strength to move forward when we are tired and to overcome obstacles that seem insurmountable. Always moving – that is *lech lecha*. This inescapable movement is referred to in the holy kabbalistic works as periods of racing out (*ratzo*) and return (*shov*). These are perpetual states of motion, always alternating back and forth. There is no stasis.

My teachers often reminded me that if a person isn't moving up, he is moving down. On some level they were right. Movement is perpetual and inherently woven into the fabric of our nature and creation, like salmon swimming upstream, going with the current or against it. This is a world of running and leaving, coming and returning, in and out. That is the pattern of natural life, it is the ebb and flow of our breath, and the pattern we are destined to follow.

But where are we going? It seems that the call to keep going, striving, and growing has become deafening. And on the surface, what could possibly be wrong with all of this wonderful movement? But as is most often the case when we are propelled to just get "there," we often lose sight of the purpose of the journey entirely.

Lech Lecha was not the only command we received to seek out God's presence. When God commanded Moses to ascend Mount Sinai to receive the Torah, He added a puzzling directive. "And the Lord said unto Moses: 'Come up to Me into the mount and be there – *heyai sham*" (Exodus 24:12). What does the phrase "be there" add? Where else was Moses supposed to be?

This is precisely the message that God wanted to resonate most powerfully for Moshe as he ascended the mountain to receive the Torah. One can invest so much strength and effort into the *lech lecha* of climbing the mountain, and yet never experience the process of being present. At the moment that Moses received the Torah, God was commanding him to be in the moment.

If a person never simply stops to take stock, all he has is a life filled with *lech lecha* that never arrives at "*heyai sham*." "Go," says God, "and climb the highest heights. But once you arrive, I want you to really be with Me." One must dwell in the moment. That moment. Every moment.

Yes, there is a stage of moving towards one's destination – a period of *lech lecha* – but, there is a concurrent directive for traversing the path that requires no destination, a directive embodied by "just be there." "Move towards My presence and be/live in My presence. Just be with Me."

Can there ever really be a culmination to the *lech lecha* process? Can a person ever say "this is it"? The answer is of course not. We are tasked to journey onwards to the Promised Land constantly seeking and searching to reveal and uncover the infinite in this world and in ourselves. Yes, within the arduous yet meaningful journey of *lech lecha*, there is the concurrent ability to be fully present. The ability to drop into moments where life is no longer just a time of running and returning – no longer a time for becoming. Life must transform into a time for being.

Most of my psychotherapy clients react to this idea with general incredulity and frustration. While most people who have entered therapy on some level are acutely aware of a general sense of "lacking" in their lives, the rest of us proceed without searching for a way to discover meaning, even though this "condition" of emptiness is one that is also felt universally. The physical world we inhabit is one that is lacking by definition. It is no coincidence that the Hebrew word for world is *olam* from the root word *he'elem* (concealment). If one is simply living in this world, one can't help but feel like there is always something missing. This void is felt most poignantly when we are on the lookout for where we want to be next, what we need to check off on our to-do list, and what self-improvement project we seek to take on. This ever present need to be moving to the next milestone on the *lech lecha* path keeps our focus on what we are not, where we are not and what our next move will be upon arrival. Paradoxically, we are tasked to just be "there," all the while, that we are travelling on the journey.

When we are attuned to the presence that accompanies us on our journey, the journey of *lech lecha* becomes a time of being, of "just be there." The focus is not on what a person may have lost along the way, or how he could have saved some time had he taken a different route, or what will be the next stop of the journey. The focus is on entering into the moment and feeling the unbelievable joy of being. This is not the antithesis of progress or accomplishment. To the contrary, this is the embodiment of achievement.

This being is the quintessential definition of *yishuv hada'at*. There is a malady that currently afflicts so many people who enter my office, whether they are aware of it or not. They arrive after all of their hard work and striving, all of the hours, days, months and years spent in pursuit of what they believed would bring them satisfaction and happiness. And they are plagued by these feelings of "not enough," feelings of distance and coldness from the lives they've created, alienation from their loved ones and themselves. All of this stems from the root cause of never allowing oneself to just be, from spending years, or even a lifetime, with the single-minded focus on "becoming," without ever once having a moment of "being."

"Being" means to stop and be filled with the presence of the moment and with "who" fills the moment. This is who I am. Now. This is who is in my life. Now. This is where I am in my education and career. Now. I accept now. I am grateful for the good that is in the now. Being fully present to what is happening precisely at this moment means not getting drawn after the mind's wandering to what happened before the journey or fretting over what will be next. All of these transitions in our lives are movements that are only with our feet, external to our being. "Being" is that recognition that no matter what happens, no matter what has transpired and what may yet transpire, we are always standing right in, and with, the presence of God. This ultimately becomes the *tachlit* of everything. This mode of being is the beginning of our connection to authentic Judaism.

The *aleph bet*, if you will, of all Jewish faith, is this belief that even though externally a person's whole life may be a back-and-forth motion in constant flux, his essence (his soul) really is, and has always been, standing before God. A person can be running all over, all the while standing still.

There is an international bestseller written by Jon Kabat-Zinn, an extraordinary human being, entitled *Wherever You Go, There You Are*. He is absolutely right. However, the subject "you" isn't just referring to the person. "You" may also refer to You, the Godly nature that resides within a person, that never leaves a person, nor can ever be left behind. The soul never runs and hides. So a person can walk away from a place, a job, a friend, his family, or even feel estranged from himself – but he cannot walk away from the Divine.

Ye are standing this day all of you before the Lord your God: your heads, your tribes, your elders, and your officers, even all the men of Israel, your little ones, your wives, and thy stranger that is in the midst of thy camp, from the hewer of thy wood unto the drawer of thy water; that thou shouldest enter into the covenant of the Lord thy God – and into His oath – which the Lord thy God maketh with thee this day.

(Deuteronomy 29:9–11)

Today a person is standing – this day. "Standing" is the act of being fully present by just standing still, by simply being. The knowledge that we are constantly standing in God's presence may terrify, cause disbelief, or just be too daunting to think about; but, in truth, it is really the most poignant expression of divine compassion and loving concern. Here and now. Always and forever.

Every time a person opens up the Pentateuch (*Chumash*) and reads these words, they will always say, "You are standing here today." And like everything else written in the Torah, "today you are standing" is an eternal message. Every time a person contemplates this verse, he can realize that "today" is referring to precisely this moment, no matter where he finds himself, at that moment.

This is a truly radical notion, because what this means for ourselves is that there is absolutely no impediment to change and spiritual growth. Today can be different – but not because a person put on a new dress, started a new relationship, or moved to the West Coast. Those actions are merely external reflections of this desire for change. And while they may lead to some form of temporary relief or progress, the gains achieved usually don't last longer than a tank of gas. But at this minute, without moving an iota, or even getting a new haircut, without doing anything, everything can change. Because to achieve this awareness, there is nothing that needs to be done. Nothing stands in the way of attaining the consciousness of the divine in the moment.

There will be times when you will hear that ever-present voice in your head reminding you that your past behavior is the best predictor of future behavior, so the likelihood of "real" change is slim to none. "Who am I to believe that after all I've been through and done I can truly change?" This debilitating question is so self-defeating that it brings about the disheartened emotional response signaling that you've given up before you even attempt to proceed.

The response to this doubting question is precisely the admonition of the Torah which serves as a constant reminder to "just stand still." In truth, there is no "where" to which a person needs to go. There is nowhere you need to run. You may feel so distanced, having journeyed far away from where you know you belong. Despite all of these doubts, the simple truth is that nothing has changed. What and who you are before the journey remains the same. "You" are still here. That person has never really left. Because God has never left that person, never left you.

Consciously (or more often subconsciously) a person might feel excluded or unworthy. He might feel as if he has done irreparable damage to his relationship with God. The verse therefore includes everyone, from the leaders to the lowliest of workers, switching from the plural to the singular, from the collective nation to its individual parts. It is true, encompassing, and it is speaking to you and me.

The way back isn't about reversing one's path. We don't retrace our steps to see where we veered off. It is about forging a new path, starting right from where we are, where we have always been. Resting in that knowledge that this moment is the departure point for connecting to the truth of our existence. And the next moment and the next and the next.

The entire process of Jewish prayer is essentially constructed around the need to "be here now." Anyone who has attended a traditional Jewish prayer service will tell you it lacks order. There is mumbling, some chanting, the occasional singing and swaying, but very little clear order or cohesiveness. But when the congregants reach the *amidah* prayer, they stand silent, wrapped in awe and personal communion.

The process of Jewish prayer, as disorganized as it may seem to even the initiated, leads a person to see himself standing together with others in the presence of the Divine. That is the intent of our prayers (in Hebrew, *kavanah,* related to *kivun,* "direction"). A person's goal is to reach this state of simply being with the Divine Presence; of being. That is where we are heading. The *lech lecha,* the journey, of the prayer service is a way of reaching the state of *amidah* – literally, "standing" – being and standing in God's presence.

The *amidah* prayer becomes a transformational moment in which the journey towards *becoming* is transformed into *being,* because a journey must have an end, and one needs the voyage in order to arrive. Each one – the becoming and the being – is necessary, but not sufficient on its own.

The sages teach that "whoever does not connect 'redemption' [as the introductory prayers are referenced in the rabbinic literature] to the *amidah* is comparable to someone who loves the king and desires very greatly to see him [and travels great distances] until he finally arrives at the entrance of the royal chamber and knocks on the door. But the king opens the door only to find that the man has fled."

Doesn't this parable elicit feelings of pity for this poor traveler? This individual, lovesick for the king, who sacrificed and endured so much to be with him, disappears right before the moment of union with the object of his desire. And if we think about it a little deeper, it wouldn't be that much of a stretch to replace this hapless nameless traveler in the story with you or me.

A person can traverse through the prayer service, the daily routines of life, the entire *lech lecha,* and finally reach the door of the King. He can believe in God, declare his oneness and omniscience, accept upon himself all of the rules and stipulations and keep the details of Jewish law meticulously. He may give charity and keep kosher. But when the King opens the door for this person (because the King very much desires to be with this person who has spent all this time and effort in the *lech lecha* stage), and says, "I hear the voice of My beloved knocking" *(Song of Songs* 2:8), he finds the doorway empty. Too caught up in the voyage, the traveler fails to arrive.

If we are unable to juxtapose and intertwine these two things, the becoming and the being, the journey and the purpose, then the tragedy of that failure to take the "redemption" and join it to the *amidah* will become a primary source of confusion and suffering – or worse, a life of never even realizing this schism and the inevitable numbness that accompanies it. This is what contributes to all of the angst and ennui that plague our often externally prosperous yet internally parched generation. The fruit has been once again separated from the tree. But here the fruit is tossed away callously as we strive to attain the next box to check off on our to-do list.

With every good deed we do, every kind word we say, and every compassionate gesture we make, we are knocking on the door to the King's palace. They are all keys to the inner sanctum, allowing us the privilege and pleasure of being with the true object of desire in this world. We are standing at the threshold of the King's palace door, and yet all this time we never actually go inside. We are stuck in a *doing* mode and too preoccupied to enter a *being* mode. But the objective of all of these commandments is precisely the *being* and not the *doing*. "I am keeping kosher." Why? "I am observing the Sabbath." Why? Why do you keep any of these laws and ultimately why are you a Jew? The whole *lech lecha* is for the purpose of being with God, of "*heyai sham*," of dwelling in the stage of being with God. But as long as this dissonance remains, and the struggle to keep moving is the main propulsion in life, a person will never be able to rest in the Presence and just be with the One to whom he is traveling and to whom he is eternally linked.

A Story

There was a certain Hasid who had been putting off a visit to his *rebbe*, the *tzaddik*, because he couldn't find a few days when he would be free to make the trip. He was an important businessman and his obligations did not allow him to go off on this less-than-pressing trip. Eventually his guilt got to him and he decided that he would go for the Sabbath but leave immediately after it was over. So he went. But whereas he would have typically received a warm welcome and a friendly greeting, this time the rebbe barely acknowledged him. Stung, the Hasid asked, "Rebbe, is everything ok?" The rebbe responded, "A Hasid who cannot stay until Sunday doesn't need to be here on Shabbat either." (How did the rebbe know? Because he was the rebbe!)

The Hasid said with an immediate change of heart, "Rebbe, I am here for as long as the rebbe says." And then the rebbe greeted him warmly. That Shabbat at the Third Meal (*shalosh se'udot*) the rebbe taught, "And the Lord said unto Moses: 'Come up to Me to the mount and be there.' What does the addition of 'be there' serve? Where else was he supposed to be?"

The rebbe continued, "Sometimes there is a Hasid who comes to the rebbe and even on the way there he is already leaving. So certainly even when he is there, he isn't there. Therefore, God says to Moses and to each and every one of us, "It is not enough to ascend the mountain. I want you to be with me."

Heard from Rav Moshe Weinberger.

Part II

Kavanot (Intentions)

$*$

T HE PRACTICE OF *YISHUV HADA'AT* should not be merely mechanical. While some "doing" is involved, *yishuv hada'at* is more appropriately an exercise in *being*. In order to sustain this practice we need to cultivate certain mindsets and attitudes: *kavanot* that enable the practice to become embodied in our daily lives. These *kavanot* form the conditions through which the practice of *yishuv hada'at* may flourish. Much like a garden requires sunlight, the gentle rains and proper environmental conditions, these mindsets are critical for connecting to the Divine in the moment. Additionally, these *kavanot* allow one to contend with the times when, on the surface, the conditions for *yishuv hada'at* appear difficult.

The fostering of *yishuv hada'at* requires both internal and external conditions of support. This section focuses on the necessary internal conditions. The *kavanot* that are described in the following chapters are by no means exclusive and independent. Rather they serve to support one another and are deeply interconnected. Practicing awareness in one will lead to the development and the deepening of others. Though this practice may require new ways of looking at our lives, including the obstacles we inevitably encounter, with practice they will form the foundation from which *yishuv hada'at* flourishes. Once firmly established, these *kavanot* will deepen and enrich the *avodah* of living a life of presence and connectivity.

Chesed: Loving-Kindness

J UDAISM IS A RELIGION of kindness, concomitant with service and Torah. Its cornerstone and foundation is, has been, and always will be loving-kindness (*chesed*). The psalmist writes, "The world was built on kindness" (Psalms 89:3). Kindness sustains and uplifts the entire world. It is the intentional alpha and omega contained within all of our actions.

You might be shaking your head, because while this sounds great in theory, Jewish law, with its strict adherence to the minutest of details, doesn't really seem to jibe with the freedom from rules and restrictions that are commonly associated with loving-kindness. At times the Torah feels more like Puritanical England than Haight-Ashbury in the 1960s.

I am struck in my own life by how my focus on performance of religious activities sometimes appears to remove me from a focus on the essential reason for performing them. I rigidly dwell on methodologies for performing the *mitzvah* properly without stopping to think about why I am doing it and what efforts my obsessive need to get it done might be. Procedure supersedes purpose.

Chesed, like most Hebrew words in this book, is difficult to translate into English. It is often rendered as loving-kindness, mercy, or great kindness. And while these are passable definitions, the most accurate definition of *chesed* according to tradition is "the unbridled desire to give, even to one who has not earned the gift." And since "the world is built upon loving-kindness," this attribute is the de facto cornerstone of all Creation.

The Talmud recounts: "It once happened that a non-Jewish individual came before Shammai and said to him, 'Make me a proselyte on the condition that you teach me the whole Torah while I stand on one foot.' Thereupon Shammai chased him away with the builder's measuring stick that was in his hand. When this man came before Hillel and asked Hillel to teach him the entire Torah while he stood on one foot, Hillel replied, 'What is hateful to you, do not do to your neighbor. That is the whole Torah; the rest is commentary. Now go and learn'" (*Talmud Shabbat* 31a).

Is that all? The whole Torah summed up in fortune cookie fashion? The answer, quite emphatically, is yes. There are no complicated theorems and algorithms. God is an absolute simple unity that our dualistic minds resist with vigor. However, our faith compels us to accept this simplistic reduction. The whole Torah can succinctly be expressed as a command to love. All else is mere commentary.

Hillel's response to the searching individual was a veiled reference to the commandment, "And you shall love your neighbor as yourself" (Leviticus 19:18). This commandment presupposes that one indeed must love his/her own self to fulfill the obligation. This cannot be emphasized enough. Self-love is an absolute prerequisite to loving another. If a person doesn't love himself unconditionally, then ultimately the love he gives will result in a loss of boundaries, not to mention a futile and agonizing search for intimacy.

Somehow, contained in this directive to love oneself and to love others in the same way is the foundation of the entire Torah. Much like the architectural designs of the world, which were designed from *chesed*, the blueprint for living in this world is one of love and unbridled giving, freely bestowed irrespective of reward.

The roots of this elemental attitudinal quality are derived from the first Jew, Abraham, who was the beginning of both the history and the soul of our people. And because everything is contained and latent in the beginning, every descendant of Abraham contains his metaphysical, spiritual DNA. And although this genetic makeup is undetectable under a microscope, it is a spiritual inheritance that all Jews share. The basic DNA of Judaism is loving-kindness.

The mystical works identify Abraham as the chariot of *chesed*. He is the archetype of this attribute, personifying it through his life's work, creating a channel to access God that had never before existed. However, it was no mere coincidence that the human being who personified this attribute of *chesed* was the first to discover the presence of the true God in the world.

God is described as being compassionate and merciful but also wrathful and even jealous. All of these anthropomorphisms don't describe God in His essence (which can never be known). Rather, these are all attributes through which His will manifests itself in this world. Yet there is one characteristic that is more Godly than all of the others, one attribute that rings truest in describing God.

> For if you keep all these commandments that I command you to do, to love *Hashem*, your God, to walk in all His ways and to cleave to Him, God will drive out all these nations from before you. (Deuteronomy 11:22–23)

After Moses warns the Jewish people to keep the *mitzvot*, love God, and walk in His ways (i.e., to be moral and perfect one's personal character traits), the verse defines the spiritual pinnacle a Jew can reach as the act of cleaving to God.

The Talmud is bothered by this directive. What could the verse possibly mean by commanding us to cleave to God? Is something like this even possible? God is a consuming fire. How can someone ever hope to hold onto an all-encompassing flame? Rather, the Talmud explains this to mean that a person must attach himself to, and emulate, the Divine characteristics. "Just as the Lord clothes the naked, so you shall clothe the naked. Just as He visits the sick, so you shall visit the sick. Just as the Lord comforted the bereaved, so you shall also comfort the bereaved; just as He buried the dead, so you shall bury the dead" (*Talmud Sota* 14a).

How can we attach ourselves to something that cannot be held? We can only do so by letting go of our own egotistical desires and focus solely on others. The greatest way to resemble the Master of the world is to perform acts of loving-kindness. Study and worship are critical parts of Divine service, but the most sublime, the most Godly, is engaging in acts of *chesed*. And while kindness is not uniquely Jewish, it infuses all of Judaism with its light and truth.

What makes *chesed* so unique that through it one can experience Divinity? The power of *chesed* and its inimitable ability to replicate the Divine derives solely from its absolutely unique characteristic that it requires no stimulus. If you were to see a homeless orphan freezing in the cold, your compassion (*rachamim*) would be aroused, and you would respond accordingly. You would sense a lack, a void, and you would need to fill it by taking action. Once this need is addressed, your compassion is no longer required. It returns to its state of dormancy. That doesn't mean that you aren't a compassionate person per se. It just means that compassion needs something external to evoke it and prompt action. The same would be true for *din*, strict judgment. If someone behaves in an inappropriate, undisciplined fashion, causing hurt or damage in a reckless manner, your sense of judgment demands that order be restored. Your response is impelled by an external stimulus.

Chesed is altogether different. The essence of *chesed* is characterized by the fact that it does not depend on anyone else. It is not a response and there is nothing and no one who can compel it. It is a state of being. It is a pure, unadulterated desire to give, whether or not there is a recipient to give to, or, more important, whether or not the recipient is deserving.

When God gives, He isn't doing so because he was asked to or because someone needs or deserves. He does so because it is how He truly relates to the world. There is an ever-increasing wellspring of *chesed* that constantly bubbles and bursts forth from the source. *Chesed*, unlike all of the other divine attributes, is not a response. It is a state of being. Therefore, it has no limit. Whatever comes as a response to something else will ultimately end once that need has been fulfilled. *Chesed* however, is innate – it comes from within. It can therefore be both endless and boundless. So if you want to truly cleave to God, like God you have to become an all-consuming fire, giving without end. By becoming a person who performs acts of kindness (*gomeil chesed*), you resemble God in the most profound way. You are transformed into a creator, a giver, someone whose desire to give is not simply to fill the need of the other outside yourself, but someone whose depths roar from within with a "flowing river," a *nachal novea* (Proverbs 18:4), a wellspring of giving. Such a person of kindness (a *baal chesed*) is, in his essence, akin to God, who is never changing and always bestowing.

An innate capacity to perform acts of loving-kindness regardless of outcome or recipient is our primary gift from God and inheritance from Abraham. This potential that rests within each and every single one of us remains unscathed, untouched and unsullied by anything we might have said or done in the past. It is our spiritual core. It remains as potent and authentic as it was on the day we were born. And it is our refuge to which we can always return, no matter what may have transpired in our lives. To access this ability doesn't require looking outside. It just requires looking inward and sharing our blessings with others. Cultivating the trait of giving without hope or expectation of recompense or appreciation, or even gratitude, is a pathway to *yishuv hada'at*.

> These are the generations of the heaven and of the earth when they were created, on the day that *Hashem* God made earth and heaven. (Genesis 2:4)

The commentators note that this verse makes use of a rare passive form of the word for creation (*behibaram* – "when they were created"), which in Hebrew is spelled with the same letters that form the name Abraham. This unique term induced our sages to make the following enigmatic statement: "God created the heavens and the earth in the merit of Abraham."

This is much more than simple word play. As already mentioned, *chesed* is the root and source of creation: "the world is built on loving-kindness." It is a necessity woven into the fabric of creation. Since the world was created through and from loving-kindness (creation, in fact, being the ultimate act of loving-kindness) and is sustained continuously through loving-kindness, it goes without saying that the name of Abraham – who is our beginning, root and source – will necessarily be found together with creation.

It might appear anomalous to attribute the creation of the universe to the merit of Abraham, who was born eons later, but Abraham's being "first" was not just in chronological terms. His being first means that he is the means through which we can attach ourselves to the loving-kindness in God and experience its presence. It's the closest we can ever get. Abraham embodied this trait irrespective of what was happening around him. Similarly, we have all been bequeathed with this ability to be our truest selves when we strive to become boundless sources of *chesed*.

This is the message that Hillel shared with the proselyte. Every commandment is a means of attaching oneself to God in the present moment, a device to come closer. But there is one most pristine form in which this can occur – and that is through *chesed*. Bring to mind a time when you performed an act of kindness. Now remember how you felt. Consider how thinking about it makes you feel, even now.

And this is what the portion of Abraham that resides in each one of us whispers constantly. No matter how far a person strays from his "true self," no matter how sullied his appearance has become or to what unhealthy and destructive point his lifestyle has degenerated, at the root there is an immutable desire to cast and share light – because at the root of the Jewish people and subsequently in each plant, branch, and leaf, is the characteristic of loving-kindness. And that point indicates that there is an essence of God at the root of each one of us. It is immutable. It cannot be affected by the conditions of the world, because it does not respond to anything external. Our urge toward *chesed* cannot be diminished. This quality, which is our birthright, has the ability to restore us to our natural state of union and communion with God, who is our home. And whereas genes can be spliced or mutated, this legacy remains ours forever.

A Reflection on the Eternal Spark of Judaism Within

Although evil influences may corrupt a Jewish soul and alienate him from his roots, a Jew is never lost. This is what our forefather Abraham was able to influence for all generations. In spite of a person feeling truly distant and removed, in the deepest recesses of the soul there resides a tiny spark of pure, untainted "Jewishness." From such a spark a brilliant flame can be rekindled. This indestructible "point" of Jewishness was implanted into the genetic design of our people by Abraham, and God promised that he would protect and preserve it forever, when he assured Abraham, "I am your shield" (Genesis 16:1). Similarly, King Solomon referred to this indestructible spark when he sang of Israel's love for God: "Although I sleep, my heart is still awake" (Song of Songs 5:1). We should bear this assurance in mind when reciting the blessing, *Magen Avraham*, Shield of Abraham.

(Chiddushei HaRim: Sefer Hazechut, Parshat Tazria)

Hitchadshut: Renewal

TO OUR MINDS, SLAVERY is an artifact of the past. While slavery has not been abolished throughout the world, it has certainly faded from contemporary Western consciousness. Yet most people do not realize that slavery very much exists. More jarring is the fact that the same people who believe slavery to have been abolished are themselves slaves! Now of course this can't be literal. Isn't a person free to do what he wants? No one is forced to act against his will!

But are we truly free? While there is a strong likelihood that you have never been systematically subjugated, who hasn't felt that he exercises little power over his choices and behaviors? The people who enter my office tend to have internalized some sort of predeterministic attitude to their choices of behaviors. "I can't change" is perhaps the most disenfranchising and confining thought a person can have. (Included in this line of thinking are "My life can't change," "Everything I do is wrong," "This situation will never get better".) Subsequently, the behaviors stemming from this mindset appear to be those of someone who is not truly free. As a person struggles with a recent loss, the pressures of family or job, the prospect of another failed relationship, or the doldrums of another seemingly empty day, that sense of being trapped or stuck reflects more a life of confinement than the freedom we claim to have.

Can you think of a time when you felt you simply had no choice? The justifications people have offered me for their unwise choices include "My father had a temper," "I don't know how to feel good without a drink," and "I hate that I am an anxious person, but my anxiety is beyond my control." These beliefs are all byproducts of this subconscious but pervasive and damaging mindset.

Thousands of years ago the Jewish people were also enslaved. Their servitude was by all accounts not only a physical subjugation but also something that affected their mind, body and soul. In truth, the Kabbalistic works speak primarily about the effects of the subjugation of the mind and spirit rather than the physical bondage.

A people that for centuries had been beaten and battered and knew nothing other than servitude were, however, ultimately destined to be redeemed, and that redemption had to first and foremost redeem them from the pervasive mindset that this enslavement had caused.

The moment of redemption began precisely when God commanded Moses to tell the Jews that they were no longer slaves but rather free men, free to worship the God of their fathers. Once their minds were free, the rest was an inevitable process.

Remarkably, nothing actually changed geographically or physically with this announcement. Even in the middle of Egypt, the transformation into a free people was already transpiring – all through one directive, the first *mitzvah* ever given to the Jewish people as a nation, which had concealed within it the key to unlock them and their descendants from the shackles of servitude, not only then but for eternity:

> This month is *to you* the first of the months.   (*Exodus* 12:1)

Practically speaking, the commandment to enumerate the months enabled the Jewish courts to establish the new months and consequently the holidays. On a deeper, more personal level, this first *mitzvah* given to the Jewish people as a whole was the commandment to "rule over time." The new month and the symbolism of the moon's perpetual cycle is the physical manifestation of the recurring spiritual phenomena that occur every single moment of our lives. But why do we need a commandment for naturally occurring phenomena? There has to be more.

The commandment to establish the new moon is really the charge for the renewal of every moment of our lives. This was not a haphazard choice as the first commandment to the Jewish people as a whole. The mystics explain that the Torah's first usage of a word serves as its archetype in the light of which all of its subsequent usages should be viewed. This axiom applies here as well. As the first commandment, the mandate to live with *hitchadshut* ("renewal") demonstrates a latent quality that defines Judaism and underlies all of its commandments: humanity's constant renewal and beginnings, our constant re-creation and connection to our Divine nature. No longer would time control us; we would be masters over time.

Our first exposure as a nation to God's will and to His Torah was the beginning of something truly radical. We were being given the taste, the first glimpse, of our own role as a free people and as individuals. The moon, unlike the sun, does not cancel the darkness that surrounds it. The night continues, despite the presence of light. The moon symbolizes the idea that even in a person's own place of darkness, regardless of what has transpired in his life, he can still feel and connect to the light. In Egypt, a place that embodied personal and national bondage, as the Jews were surrounded by what felt like an abyss of despair, that tiny speck of light of the present moment symbolized a new beginning. Even during the plague of darkness, the Jews in Goshen had light; darkness abounds, but it is not destiny. There was no dramatic fanfare or grandeur when God presented this – rather, the simple message that in the midst of the darkness a person can still feel the opportunity for renewal and change: the gift of transformation. This was something new, revolutionary – but most important, this was our liberation. Our entrance and first exposure to the Torah while still enslaved in Egypt offered us the key to escape servitude then and for time everlasting.

The Jews had never completely lost their faith or their identities as a separate people. They knew that they were the children of Abraham, Isaac and Jacob. However, they lacked the clarity and precision to know that the freedom to change, to transcend time, resided within them. And the only way was through a direct encounter with this moment. The first commandment had to be the sanctification of the now, because only this moment transcends the bonds of time.

Redemption (*geulah*) makes a person free. He is no longer enslaved. Just because things have been a certain way for a period of time does not mean that he cannot change. When God wanted to free the Jewish people from Egypt, He first had to instruct them on the meaning of freedom, how to truly be free. By giving the commandment to sanctify the new moon, God was revealing the essence of freedom and the means to redemption. The gift of the present is that it ultimately provides true freedom (*cherut*). In truth, a person is

79

not enslaved to his passions, his fears, his shortcomings, even though he has a history of surrendering to them, because right now he is free. The idea so eloquently expressed by Viktor Frankl that "every human being has the freedom to change at any instant" is the secret of the redemption. This is what God had to teach the Jewish people from the abyss. And this is what we can return to anytime we are once again shackled in the chains of mental slavery. History is not destiny. Habit is not destiny. Addiction is not destiny.

It should therefore come as no surprise how often the Torah commands us to remember the Exodus. The Torah's wisdom is not some form of archaic laws and rules but instead a vibrant and contemporary guide to our lives. We are commanded to remember the Exodus because we need to constantly bring ourselves back to the present moment. Our liberation transcended the physical dimension. Our Exodus was eternal. Remember that you are free. Remember how to be free. Remember that you never have to be a slave again.

A Reflection on the Immediacy of Choice

"Today, if you will but listen to His voice!"

(Psalms 95:7).

Think only about the present day and the present moment. When someone wants to begin to serve God, it seems too much of a burden to bear. But if you remember that you have only today, it won't be such a burden. Don't push off serving God from one day to the next, saying, "I'll start tomorrow – tomorrow I'll pray with real devotion and concentration."

All we have is the present day and the present moment. Tomorrow is a whole different world.

(Likutey Moharan I, 272)

Shemot: Never Forgetting Your Name

THE SECOND BOOK of the Pentateuch, the book of Exodus, tells of the Jewish people's exile and bondage in Egypt and their subsequent redemption. The Hebrew name of this book, *Shemot*, "Names," is derived from its first verse. And although there is only a limited correlation between the Hebrew names of the books of the Bible and their English counterparts (Leviticus and Vayikra anyone?), there is some coincidental truth here, because exodus – redemption – comes directly from a person remembering his name, i.e., who he is. Revelation and redemption come from never forgetting our names, never forgetting who we are.

There is a longstanding tradition within Judaism to recite a verse corresponding to the first and last letter of one's Hebrew name at the end of the *amidah* prayer. There are mystical, kabalistic reasons for this practice, but we will keep it simple. Although it is true that "a rose by any other name would smell as sweet" (Shakespeare's *Romeo & Juliet*), the emphasis placed on one's name is meant to ensure that one never forgets one's essence, one's identity. Forgetting one's name means forgetting who one really is.

Isn't that what happens when a person is depressed? He forgets who he is, what he can do, his identity and his abilities. What he is capable of doing in his life has become distorted. His understanding of the people around him is inaccurate, and the world and its inhabitants have become his enemies. He grows distanced from himself and from his surroundings. To put this all succinctly, a person living with depression has forgotten his name and becomes someone or something else. Successful treatment restores his name to him and him to his name.

Now these are the names of the sons of Israel, who came into Egypt with Jacob; every man came with his household.
(Exodus 1:1)

Once again we return to the idea that the beginning of anything contains its essence, its soul. The first verse therefore contains the *neshama* of the entire book. The entire book of Exodus, its meaning – past, present, and future – is contained therein. There is something about the names that contains the key to the entire redemption. The midrash – the rabbinical oral tradition – comments on this verse that in the merit of the Jewish people not having changed their names in exile they were worthy of redemption. The midrash's comment is not simply a matter of formality and tradition. The main impetus for redemption is for a person to remember his name. Indeed, the entire redemption was contingent on the Jews having not changed their names. In spite of all the changes and difficulties of their lives of servitude in Egypt, the Jews stayed with their names. Somehow in the midst of their oppressive lives they were able to remember their names.

The whole rectification of the redemption from Egypt came as a result of remembering. The Hebrew word for Egypt, *Mitzrayim*, means "constraint" and "constriction." Indeed, the slavery was back-breaking and arduous, but it is not the physical work that enslaves a person. Only when a person forgets who he really is can he become a slave.

The Baal Shem Tov teaches that exile means forgetting. Therefore, redemption must de facto mean remembering. The worst thing to forget is one's "I." A person who forgets who he truly is, is exposed to the most painful exile possible: exile from himself. The whole point of the backbreaking work was to make the lives of the Jews bitter. But the bitterness of slavery doesn't have to take away a person's name. Pharaoh wanted us to not only be subservient, but to forget as well. He employed this stratagem ruthlessly, as have all of the persecutors of the Jewish people. It was not too long ago that numbers were branded onto the arms of Jews to depersonalize them and supplant their names. This was done specifically in order that they should forget their names, forget who they truly are. Unfortunately, this ruse is not only perpetrated by anti-Semitic adversaries. This is a deception that we employ against ourselves.

"The curious paradox is that when I accept myself just as I am, then I can change," writes Carl Rogers. There needs to be an unconditional acceptance that predicates any genuine growth. Without fully being able to see oneself, there is no amount of "self-help" that can motivate or assist a person to leave his or her own personal Egypt. The actual translation of the first verse of Exodus is: "These are the names of the children of Israel *who are coming* into Egypt." The usage of the present progressive tense indicates that the sons of Jacob are coming into Egypt right now. At first glance, this expression would have been more appropriate when the Torah described their actual arrival in Egypt, when they were in the process of entering, and not in its recapitulation of the story, when the children of Jacob had already been in Egypt for centuries. The Torah was simply reviewing what had happened previously. So why choose the misleading wording that makes it seem as if the Jewish people had just now entered into exile?

This description of the Jewish people as they were on the cusp of redemption is indeed puzzling, but it is a central theme of the Book of Exodus. Our introduction to their imminent exodus, the moment they are about to leave, the moment they are about to be redeemed, is described as the moment that they have just arrived (or are just arriving). How is it possible that at the very moment of redemption, the beginning of freedom, the people's predicament is described as if they had just entered, or are entering into, exile?

The Torah is neither a story book nor a history. The word "Torah" means teaching. So this strange formulation must be designed to cultivate a constant awareness of a basic truth. The lesson to which the Torah wants to sensitize us, is that even when a person is in exile (distanced from himself) and appears to be undergoing cataclysmic changes in his life – be they religious, historical, socio-political, economic, romantic – none of those changes that are occurring touch upon the essence of the person.

The names of the Jewish people identify not who these people are biographically and historically but their essential nature. The names are symbolic and revelatory of their true essence, their unadulterated, pristine spirit. Egypt was the paradigm of all future possible exiles – national and personal – and all were said to be contained in the exile of Egypt. In spite of the fact that the Jewish people would in the future be forced to endure exiles and adopt foreign behaviors and mannerisms, at times compelled to behave or think in ways completely antithetical to their values, they would always be able to retain this inalienable connection to their essence, just as they did in Egypt. This is the deeper meaning of the statement that the names of the Jews in Egypt never changed. A person can act in so many ways that make him feel completely alienated from who he really is, but his name, the identity, the vital, central, essential core part of him, remains the same. If a person does not cultivate this awareness, he risks being lost in Egypt forever.

Even now, after the many years of being in Egypt, the inner reality and essence of the Jewish people remained the same. It is as if this day and moment, or every day and moment, the Jews entered into exile. And that allows for the possibility of redemption. Whatever the nature of the exile – whether it's the hundreds of years of slavery, or years of addiction, the seemingly endless cycles of depression, can seem far too burdensome to overcome. But something that just occurred may immediately be reversed. This awareness can be evoked anytime a person feels as if he is in physical exile or, more painfully, in a state of internal separation. Even when a person is feeling displaced and exiled from himself, his identity can never fully be one with the "Egypt" to which he currently feels enslaved. In spite of his past failures and disappointments, his inner name is immutable. After all of the experiences that a person undergoes, the essence of who he is never changes. On a superficial level, a person can feel very comfortable in the mindless state of the exile of forgetfulness. But there is always a longing for something true, the remembrance of who he really is. Only when this idea is internalized can the existential itch be scratched.

In every single generation and every single day, a person must envision himself as if today he left Egypt. It is not enough for this obligation to be fulfilled as a yearly reminder on Passover, the holiday that commemorates the exodus from Egypt. The Lubavitcher Rebbe deftly points out that the only way it is possible for a person to remember that he is leaving Egypt every day is if, at some point, he had slipped right back into Egypt! (You can't "leave" a place without having been there to begin with.) If we are obligated to do this every day, then it means that we are tasked to always be aware that we have the capacity to redeem ourselves from the Egypt that we have slipped back into, from the slaveries of our daily existence.

Every time we "forget" is another instance where we have fallen back into Egypt. When a person forgets that he is more than his desires, more than his inadequacies, when he forgets that he is not imprisoned within his physical limitations, he has slipped back into exile. But that exile is only a temporary state. Even after years of self-neglect and disregard, it is still as if he just arrived in Egypt, because his essence has not changed. The moment of redemption, the moment of freedom, comes from the moment of this remembering.

It was for this specific reason that the Sages established that the reading of the Exodus of Egypt be connected to the recital of the *Shema* prayer: "Hear O Israel, the Lord is our God, the Lord is One." *Shema* is the declaration of presence, the opportunity to free ourselves from the servitude of Egypt, from the delusion of the restricted consciousness of Egypt, and bring ourselves into the awareness of the kingship of God, each and every day. *Shema* is the recognition that there is a Godly part within each and every one of us. And when that essential piece is brought into the field of consciousness, all bonds of slavery dissipate. This is not a one-time occurrence. This is an obligation anytime our forgetfulness brings us back down to Egypt. And the moment of our remembering is always accompanied by our redemption. When we are cognizant that we are servants of the one God, it is hardly possible to be enslaved to any other thing.

It is with this recognition that we praise God each morning upon our awakening. The tired soul that through the course of the previous day has inevitably once again ended up in Egypt, in the straits, in the ditches, is once again renewed – not refurbished or patched-up with a new coat of paint but a pure, unblemished, brand-new soul, because that state of unconsciousness is temporary, and all it takes is a moment's recognition to revert back to the true state, pure, unsullied, and pristine. Regardless of the *Mitzrayim* experience you have gone through or may even be currently going through today, right now, at this moment, you can leave. You haven't been stuck for the past ten years, because today you came into Egypt, which means that you can leave that uncharacteristic, temporary, superficial exile. No matter what has transpired and in spite of the habits and mannerisms that you have developed, the unalienable reality is that today you came into Egypt. Your *Mitzrayim* experience can never be identified with the essence of who you are. This servitude is foreign to you as soon as you recognize it. Immediately, a person who is at the lowest rung of the ladder, someone who has hit rock bottom, can be transformed, precisely because the essential part of who he is never left him.

The Talmud tells that after a person's death his soul is asked questions about how it conducted itself while it inhabited the body. One of those questions is, "Were you longing for redemption?" That question presupposes the recognition and belief that each one of us is worthy of redemption at any given moment. On both a national and individual level, every moment we are worthy. How else can a person honestly answer that question in the affirmative and say that, yes, he was always awaiting? You must have the capacity for redemption in order to await it.

While there is no denying the external damage and deficiencies which are a necessary part of the human condition, inwardly we are all pure and clean. But if a person does not believe this, if he does not believe in the connection he has with his name, if he does not look at his exiled self as an external façade, then he cannot possibly be awaiting redemption at that moment. Every Jew is obligated to see himself as if he personally exited Egypt. This is not an exercise in fantasy; it is the ultimate reality. Each of us, by living in the present, and choosing how we relate to that reality, leaves Egypt every moment of every day. Every moment is a new opportunity for a person to assert this belief, to redeem himself from all that surrounds him and to ultimately redeem his "self."

A Reflection on One's Essential Nature

In every generation and every day a person is obliged to regard himself as if he had that day come out of Egypt . . . and in particular through accepting the Kingdom of Heaven during the recital of the *Shema*, wherein the person explicitly accepts and draws upon himself G-d's unity, when he says: 'The Lord is our G-d, the Lord is One'. . . . 'Therefore nothing stands in the way of the soul's unity with G-d and His light, except one's will; for should the person not desire at all, G-d forbid, to cleave to Him. . . . But immediately when he does so desire, and accepts and draws upon himself His blessed G-dliness and declares: "The L-rd is our G-d, the L-rd is One," then surely his soul is spontaneously absorbed into G-d's unity, for "spirit evokes spirit and draws forth spirit." And this is a form of "Exodus from Egypt." Therefore, it was ordained that the paragraph concerning the Exodus from Egypt be read specifically during the recital of the *Shema*, even though it is a commandment by itself, not pertaining to the commandment to recite the *Shema*, as stated in the Talmud and Codes, for they are actually the same thing.

(*Tanya*, Chapter 47)

Shiviti: Equanimity

E VERY SPIRITUAL PATH is fraught with difficulty, and the Jewish path is no different. More often than not, what stands in the way of our spiritual aspirations are our own internal struggles and upheavals rather than any external impediment to growth. The insidious impediments our own minds create often prove to be the most difficult and arduous to overcome.

King David writes, "I have set (*shiviti*) God before me at all times" (Psalms 16:8). The Baal Shem Tov, the pioneer of the Hasidic movement, deviates from the traditional interpretation by explaining that the word *shiviti* connotes an expression of *hishtavut* ("equanimity," "equilibrium"), a state in which the response to all stimuli – for instance whether a person is praised or shamed, will always be consistent and measured, one of balance and steadiness. For, regardless of circumstances, viewed in the proper perspective they are all essentially the same. A balanced individual with a balanced mind might be swayed momentarily but quickly regains his or her footing. Such a person remains the person that he or she is.

This attitude seems almost too good to be true. So much of our self-worth is predicated on how others view us. We seek and sometimes crave the approval of our spouse, boss, co-workers, or friends, while being careful to shy away from the people who with a single critical comment or a fleeting glance of disapproval might throw us into complete disarray. Subconsciously, much of our lives are spent vacillating between seeking the approval of others, all the while being careful never to expose ourselves to situations when our sense of "ok-ness" can be stripped from us. Is it even realistic for a person to somehow hope to inoculate himself from the constant upheaval and disappointment deriving from a world in which "every day's curse is worse than that of the previous day" (*Sotah* 49a)? The Baal Shem Tov suggests that, in spite of difficulties to achieve balance in a world that is constantly spinning out of control, we are able to access a deeper calm akin to the placid waters that lie beneath the churning surface of the ocean whose crashing waves are powerless to affect the peaceful depths.

When I discuss this topic with my patients, I find that most people's initial reaction to this description is that it appears to be promoting the idea that they adopt an attitude of remote detachment and apathy, to remove themselves from the realities and harsh challenges of life. They respond by asking me what benefit would be accrued by replacing their reactions, even if sometimes extreme and disturbing, with passive withdrawal, and the same modulated, unemotional reaction to every stimulus? They properly assert that these responses are neither human nor appropriate.

But they misunderstand. Cultivating the mindset and attitude of *shiviti* fully and properly allows for a person to be fully present to his thoughts and feelings, by being attuned to the unfolding nature of God's revelation in each and every moment of his life.

Cultivating this attitude of *shiviti* means that a person's every word, thought and action, in truth, every moment in his life, can be a point of departure for contemplation and an encounter with Godliness – not just when he is studying Torah, praying or meditating. The encounter with God can be constant and consistent.

A person must be careful not simply to relate to this as a profound philosophical and theological doctrine of God's immanence, allowing us to perceive and be affected by God's presence. Rather it is a guide to action, not just contemplation, regardless of the current events of that moment. This is something that holds genuine ramifications for us all. If at every moment we lived with the crystal-clear recognition that the present moment contains within it an opportunity to remove the covering from a world where God's felt presence is hidden and to clearly see that here is God, then this moment becomes one with the possibility to forge genuine connection. The results can be transformative.

Our frustrations and disappointments result directly from what we perceive to be failures to achieve what will be best for us, and what we perceive to be harm and slights done towards us. But no matter what the circumstances, no matter how dire the situation, there is always the opportunity to attach oneself to the moment, to the holiness intrinsic in each and every breath. In the face of adversity, it is an act of courage to reach out to the divinity that resides within and not allow any other factor to determine our reactions.

The inevitable result of wanting to be somewhere other than where you are or fervently wishing for a different outcome than the one received is the disappointment and frustration of rejecting the actuality of what really is happening right now. Fully attaching yourself to the present situation means that right now this is precisely where you are supposed to be, this is what you are supposed to be doing, and this is what is supposed to be happening. Now, given that, and not some fictive notion of how things should be, how should one respond? If a person is always tuned into the reality of Godliness in all things, then everything will be balanced, because it is all clearly God's will, it is all the same, and it all awaits your decision as to how to properly respond. Right now, this is how God wants to be served. Right now things are as they are supposed to be. Everything is in its right place.

So instead of inducing apathy or docile acceptance, this radical notion serves to empower us with the realization that in every moment of his life there is another unique opportunity and ability to reveal Godliness, to encounter the present with the power within. We are not being docile; we are seizing control of the moment. This should not to be confused with a passive and begrudging acceptance of God's will; rather, this is an active, vibrant acceptance of seeing things as they are, as they are meant to be seen, as a precursor to appropriate response and action. This concept goes far beyond the acknowledgement of the righteousness of God's actions in everything that transpires (which is of course a basic Jewish tenet). It offers the liberating possibility of accepting hardships and difficulties with unbridled optimism and love. It is the redemption that a person can bring to the reality within him to whatever the reality he is currently experiencing. This balance is the product of the revolutionary mindset of not living for a moment without feeling the presence of Godliness in everything that exists, together with the ability to transform this moment.

By not becoming overwhelmed by good fortune or terrible grief, a person is not numbing himself against the world. Rather, he is demonstrating a complete and utter awareness of God's constant influence upon this moment. *Hishtavut* is the clear recognition that everything transpiring, both inside and around a person, is merely a garment that clothes the source of reality. It is the living, breathing possibility for connection with each moment, and the opportunity to accept and embrace it, no matter what form it takes.

A Reflection on Stability and Equanimity

[As a gloss on the text: "These were the years of Sarah's life"]
The midrash states: "Just as they are perfect, so are their years
perfect." Rashi explains: "'The years of Sarah's life' – they were all
equally good." This is the trait of equanimity mentioned in the
book *Duties of the Heart*. It is a great virtue that a person should
stand firm in his perfection in the face of all that affects him.
There is a trial for one who is poor, and a trial for one who is
wealthy. Sarah, in her early years, lived through various difficult
periods – through hunger, through being taken by Pharaoh and
Avimelekh. And in their later years, [Avraham and Sarah] had all
that is good, but nothing changed within her character, despite
all these changes. This is what the Mishna [means when it] says:
"With ten trials was Avraham *Avinu* tested and he stood firm
through all, to show how great was the love of Avraham *Avinu*,
may he rest in peace" (Avot 5:4). This means: his great love for
the Holy One, blessed be He. All the winds in the world could
not budge him from his place. He stood firm in his perfection,
feeling nothing whatsoever of all that passed over him. Unlike
ordinary mortals who undergo several changes every day, they
never changed throughout their years. The verse states about
them: "She will do him good and not evil all the days of her life"
(Proverbs 31:12), despite all kinds of vicissitudes and trials, in
poverty and in wealth.   (*Sefat Emet, Chayyei Sara,* 5656)

"I have set (*shiviti*) the Lord always before me" (Psalms 16:8).
Shiviti is an expression of *hishtavut*, "equanimity." Whatever the
occasion, it is all the same to him, whether people are praising
him or they are humiliating him, and so too in all matters. And
similarly with everything he eats, whether he is eating delicacies,
or he is eating other things, it is all the same to him, since the
evil inclination is entirely removed from him. Whatever happens
to him, he says, "Surely this comes from Him, blessed be He,
and if in Your eyes it is fitting, etc." His every intention is for the
sake of Heaven, but from his perspective, it makes no difference.
This is a very high level.   (*Tzava'at ha-Rivash,* 2)

Temimut: Wholeheartedness

Y OU MIGHT BE FAMILIAR with the notion that we all have an "inner child" residing within. Of course this child is not a literal physical entity, but that does not detract from the very real nature of this phenomena. This inner child doesn't refer to our childlike behavioral aspects, but, rather, to our child-like capacity for presence, kindness, joy, sensitivity and kindness. Inevitably, for most people, this inner child can be buried so deeply within, that the mere notion of its existence is dismissed as juvenile fantasy or fiction and the capacities for these feelings are remote. But just as we were all once children, the capacity for experiencing life as one did as a child persists. Indeed, the disconnect from this inner child serves as a core impediment to feeling and living with *yishuv hada'at*, manifesting itself most poignantly in periods of life when a person senses being out of touch, or exiled from parts of one's own self.

The Baal Shem Tov teaches that exile means forgetting, which can only mean that redemption means remembering. (See "*Shemot:* Never Forgetting Your Name.") The worst thing to disregard, the most painful source of neglect, is, as Rav Kook writes, forgetting the "I." "I am in the midst of the exile" (Ezekiel 1:1) is how the prophet Ezekiel begins his prophecy. Ezekiel was not lamenting that he was far away from his former geographic location he had once been in. He was lamenting that his "I," his true sense of self, had been forgotten, swept up in the waves of exile.

What causes this estrangement from this vital part of our identity and self? It seems that the "noise" of life overwhelms the inner melody of the soul, "the inner child," until it cannot be heard, drowned out by the cacophonous outside commotion. Experience drowns out innocence. In a process that is often barely discernable, there occurs a subtle yet sinister progression away from this melody, which serves to confuse our deepest held values, leaving us filled with angst. Unfortunately, no one is immune from this subtle yet painful erosion. What causes this distraction? How do these impediments within become so impermeable that we are no longer able to hear the natural, healthy melody of the soul within? These blockages sever the connection with the spirituality that is all around us, along with the radiance that was and still is within, the beauty that is unsullied no matter how the past may have unfolded. What stands in the way of this voice? When did we lose touch with ourselves? And how can we restore it?

The roots of the exile of "the self" go back to the beginning, when we, in the persons of Eve and Adam, were in *Gan Eden* (the Garden of Eden). For a brief time, man was able to live with God – not with the concept of God, but actually in the felt presence of the Creator.

In this spiritual state there was no need for clothing, for nothing needed to be masked. There was nothing sexualized about the nude figure. Being without clothing meant that there was nothing forged, nothing counterfeit, and nothing that was not "me." The root of the Hebrew word for "garment," *beged*, means deceit. Beyond the practical benefits of clothing, what we wear is often the expression of how we want to present ourselves to the world in order for people to think a certain way about us. As on stage, it is our costume designed to reveal (or hide) a character. We are dressed up, "made up," disguising ourselves to the world so that it will think a certain way about us, transforming ourselves into something else. In Eden, on the other hand, nakedness meant complete and absolute self. No forgeries, no deception, no dissembling.

And then things went terribly wrong. As a result of the first sin, Adam and Eve (and we with them) were forced to leave *Gan Eden*. That cataclysmic event was prompted by the root within mankind that seduces him to separate from the source of his life, ironically, in order to "find himself," the sin of the earth that deviated from God's command. Ironically, Adam was seduced into believing that the only way to become the essential Adam, free of externalities, was by getting further away from *Gan Eden*, and further away from the voice of God, from his inner voice.

Adam tore the fruit from the tree, separating the process from the outcome, the child from the parent. (See *Back to Eden.*) "I don't want or need the tree anymore," man says, "I want the fruit. I want to be removed from the tree, the source, roots and symbol of where I come from." Whereas eating from the Tree of Life means that a person lives in constant connection with his source, eating from the Tree of Knowledge of Good and Evil reveals man's desire to believe that he will find happiness apart from his roots, his source of life. So begins this insidious process of being torn further and further from his source that began with heeding the voice of the snake and continues to this day with the subsequent call of the millions of voices from outside.

> Unto the woman He said: "I will greatly multiply thy pain and thy travail; in pain thou shalt bring forth children."
> (Genesis 3:16)

The curse of leaving Eden also constitutes the labor pains of childbirth. After Eden, bearing children hurts women. But that "labor" pain isn't reserved for just physical progeny. That pain also comes from the inability to deliver, (give birth to) the multifaceted abilities that we carry within us, the love and joy and faith and creativity, that are also our offspring. From the day that we left *Gan Eden,* giving birth to that deepest part of ourselves is going to be accompanied by tremendous pain. It will no longer be clear to us how we are to give birth or even to what we are supposed to give birth to. Our very creativity and our ability to recapture our essential happiness and productivity, becomes difficult and even painful.

> "And here the child asks."   (*Pesach Haggadah*)

One of the most timeless traditions of the Seder night is to have the youngest child present ask the Four Questions to commence the telling of the story of the Exodus from Egypt. Although it is traditional at the Pesach Seder to have only the children ask the Four Questions, according to the mystical works the real purpose of this tradition is that each person also ask himself these questions. This introduces the notion that a person must always ask himself, "What is different about this night? How can I be redeemed from exile?"

The custom – like all of our customs, rooted in the deepest mysteries and secrets of Torah – is that the youngest child should ask first. If we ourselves are asking these questions of ourselves, what does the role of the "youngest child" symbolize? Clearly it refers to that part of ourselves that is purest and most innocent, that is the part of ourselves (and indeed we all have this part) called the youngest child. It is our lost "inner child." This part is the primal essence of who we are, the part inside us that is completely unsophisticated. Ever since we lost touch with that child, we've encountered difficulties, and ever since we could no longer hear that little child asking questions, we find ourselves entangled in seemingly insoluble issues. The "I" has become buried, lost in an imitation of life, a forged sense of identity. Influenced by society, culture and advertisements, we express words, emotions and gestures that are not coming from our true essence. To one degree or another, we have become tainted and spoiled as a result of having been overwhelmed with ideas, words, images, beliefs and thoughts that are not our own. The complexity that we perceive in life and impose on ourselves obliterates the simplicity we once knew. But in spite of all of the "dead weight" we may have accumulated, there is a part of ourselves that is completely free of this forgery, a part that has retained the absolute, unblemished innocence and pureness of who we really are, the same innocence that existed in Eden when there was nothing but that simple existence. Just as, at the Seder, we are obligated to experience the Exodus from Egypt as though we ourselves participated at the infancy of the Jewish nation, so we are obligated to recover the innocence and simplicity of the children we all once were.

Why it is so important that a person needs to be aware of and listen to this youngest child? Isn't a more refined and mature perspective on life more desirable than the immature vantage point of children? We all know that "kids say the darndest things," but is there a value in doing away with the artifice and sophistication of adult expression?

The value in the natural flow that comes from a child's mouth and the reason that children are prone to say anything on their mind is because the source of their speech is the natural, flowing current of the self. There is no filter. They say exactly what they are thinking and feeling, with no ulterior motive and no subtext. And as in the case of the parents of a child who asked the man on the bus whether he had a baby in his belly, might feel this to be the cause of some embarrassment, the child is simply the vessel of a powerful, flowing current of unspoiled, natural simplicity. When he says, "I want this," there is no subterfuge. That means just that he really wants it. He is completely connected to the unadulterated self. But if you or I were to say "I want something," there are usually a few pages of fine print that go along with that request. When we use the word "I," its meaning has become so tampered with, so opaque and ambiguous. We often don't know what would be "best" for us because we have no idea who "we" are. But the child's "I"? That "I" is crystal clear.

The Talmud recounts many stories in which a great sage was faced with a dilemma. He had been called upon to resolve a burning issue, often an issue whose resolution might determine the survival and destiny of the Jewish people. The sage would search through his vast knowledge and still find himself unsettled and unable to decide what to do. In order to quell his doubt, he would do something highly unconventional. He would approach a child by happenstance on his way home from school and ask him, "Tell me what you learned today. Teach me the day's lesson." (*Medrash Rabbah Esther*: 7)

As children are wont to do, whatever sprang into his mind, would be the child's answer, and from that interaction the sage, the great leader of the generation, would decide what steps to take. And because of that serendipitous meeting, the fate of the entire community was decided.

What? Could that really be the plan? The fate of countless lives decided by a chance encounter? There must be more than meets the eye here.

Within each of us is a sage, not necessarily wise and not purely a function of intelligence. It is the sum of our experience and education, the inner, clever, educated know-it-all. Over the course of a lifetime, this clever persona has picked up a thousand different ideas, thoughts and feelings. Through the journey of life, this "sage" has amassed information, opinions and identities. Along the way though, he may have very well lost touch with his real identity.

Very often, when we are no longer able to answer the question of the youngest child, we shut the questions out. Instead we are firm in knowing how our teacher, parent, or the billboard would answer, and that suffices. We can go our entire lifetime simply regurgitating what has been said over and over and over, never once ever being able to truly attribute our words and actions to "I." When we are confronted by reality, we offer slogans and platitudes in response.

At critical moments, at a crossroads when the weight of the situation and the ramifications are too great to leave to all the information he is constantly accumulating and to the personas he has adopted, or when the contradictory weight of experience has no utility, the sage realizes that the answer lies deeper within. The sage, that part of us that is sophisticated, complex, and seemingly omniscient, is, at that point, able to consult the little, innocent, pure child inside and searching within, asks, "What do I really feel right now? What am I thinking right now? I don't know who I am anymore. I have become so caught up in dissembling to the world, I am no longer sure what I really think. What is really true right now?" The adult knows that this child does not live with the calculations and distractions of what once was and what might be in ten years. In these critical times, for the moments that demand extreme honesty, the wise man goes searching for the child inside himself – the pure, true self, the point inside that remains unadulterated by the multitude of identities superimposed on the surface – to uncover the simplicity that exists in him, as it exists in all of us.

Simplicity (*temimut*) is not stupidity. It is not remaining oblivious to what has happened in the past or what may happen in the future. Nor is it living in a hedonistic or nihilistic manner with no concerns for the future at all. It is living with an innocence and humility that come from recognizing that all a person really has is right now.

Often our minds do not allow us the freedom to consider what our lives would be like if we lived with that *temimut,* that inner child, always. The response of this inner child does not involve elaborate calculations. There is no anticipated gain. There isn't regret over recent disappointments or failures. It is a simple, clear awareness that none of these factors have true bearing on the truth of this moment. That was then, this is now. A child lives in the truth of his existence of the moment. He is, right now. Life is not so complicated that it cannot be approached from the perspective of simple truth and simple values. Most often, if we are willing to approach issues with honesty and clarity, we know what course of action is consistent with Jewish values and God's will. We just need to articulate the question and let the answer emerge from our inner child.

It is funny to see someone talking to himself. When there is nobody around, there is no need to ask questions. A person knows what he knows. However, if you watch children, they talk to themselves all the time. Self-talk is a device to express feelings and gain an understanding of one's environment. God wants there to be a relationship between the adult (the sage) and the little child inside us. That relationship can only be cultivated when a person starts to pose these questions to himself. This is the deeper meaning of a person asking himself the four questions on the night of the Seder. Even if he is alone – and in truth that is always the case – a person must ask himself over and over: "What is true right now?" and not, "What do I wish to be true?" or "What do I wish weren't so?" The question must be the simple awareness of what is, without preconceived notions and fears: "What is happening right now?" We seek the simple awareness of what is.

The child asks questions like: Who am I? Why am I here in the world? Where did I come from? What do I want to be when I grow up? What can bring meaning into my life? Regrettably, adults have stopped asking these questions. Thinking they have become sages, the child learns not to ask these questions.

With *temimut*, we can connect our inner *sod*, our innermost "secret," and access the secret of all existence. No matter what a person is involved in, be it the loftiest spiritual matters or the most mundane physical activities, he must believe in his worth, in his essence. Nothing is too small and nothing is too big if it is part of his Truth (with a capital T). The voice of the snake, the seductive voice of yet another external source, is easily dismissed when it is confronted by a voice fully connected to one's self, fully connected to one's source.

A Reflection on Simplicity

Thou shalt be whole-hearted with the Lord thy God.
(Deuteronomy 18:13)

Be wholehearted with the Lord, your God: Conduct yourself with Him with simplicity and depend on Him, and do not inquire of the future; rather, accept whatever happens to you with [unadulterated] simplicity and then, you will be with Him and part of Him. *(Sifrei)*

Happy is the man who walks the true path, avoiding all sophistication. He is "simple and upright, fearing G-d and shunning evil." (Job 1:1, 1:8, 2:3)

Many times the Rebbe said that no sophistication is needed in serving G-d. All that is required is simplicity, sincerity, and faith. The Rebbe said that simplicity is the highest possible thing. G-d is certainly higher than all else. And G-d is ultimately simple. *(Sichot Haran* 101)

Simchah: Authentic Joy

ONE OF THE OCCUPATIONAL hazards of being a psychologist is that it seems that everyone I encounter professionally wants to know why he or she isn't happy. Sometimes this request is stated explicitly, but more often implicit in their speech is a notion of desperately wanting to experience this elusive feeling, or sensing that they lack enough of it. People unfortunately make the mistake of turning this question into a binary one: "Am I happy or am I not happy?" This, however, is incorrect. There is an entirely different and better way to approach our need for more happiness in our lives.

Of course we all want to be happy. No one wakes up in the morning wanting and wishing to feel miserable. But when the Torah refers to happiness, it isn't just referring to a desirable experience with concurrent psychological benefits. *Simchah* ("joy"), unlike any other emotion, is critical to attaining and cultivating *yishuv hada'at*. And, much like *yishuv hada'at*, it is as fundamentally important to our growth and development, our survival, as breathing and eating are.

In numerous places throughout the Torah there are explicit commandments to be joyful. "Because you did not serve *Hashem* your God with joy and goodness of heart . . ." (Deuteronomy 28:47) serves as the rationale for the extensive list of punishments and suffering that will ensue as retribution for not possessing this critical character trait. However, the whole notion of being commanded to feel anything is foreign to our modern-day sensibilities. I acknowledge to my patients that no one can compel them to feel one way or another, not even the Torah's command. I often paraphrase Eleanor Roosevelt's comment to my clients, "No one can force you to feel anything without your consent."

We simply can't be told how to feel. Additionally, we can't compel ourselves to feel anything. We either feel, or we don't. How many marriages have dissolved because one or both of the parties simply stopped feeling anything? How often is there a powerful emotion that we just wished we could discard, but to no avail?

Later in the book we will discuss how, in the mystical works of Judaism, the expression that "evil does not descend from the heavens" is used to describe our relationship to emotions. Put simply, there is no such thing as a "bad" emotion. (See "*B'ruchim HaBa'im: A Reflection on Emotions*.") There is room for whatever a person is feeling. But there is also the recognition that one can't be forced or commanded to feel anything.

Presumably, if you and I know this, God knows this as well. In fact, any sort of requirement to feel anything will more often than not result in the exact opposite. Commanded to feel something other than what we are actually feeling will only result in frustration and exasperation. Told that we need to feel happy, we are left with few responses. "Do I need to be happy? Thanks for the helpful suggestion, but tell me what exactly I should be happy about? I am not happy. Maybe I used to be happy, but now my – insert cause of current distress in my life – precludes that from happening. I simply don't feel it anymore."

Nevertheless, because *simchah* is essential to a life of *yishuv hada'at*, and because it is commanded that we experience and absorb it into our own existence, it must be that *simchah* is not merely an emotion that occurs or does not occur, but an attitude, that can be developed and nurtured. One can become more physically fit by exercise and training. Similarly, one can engender within himself the *simchah* that God requires and desires. *Simchah* is a skill.

> When the month of *Av* begins, we decrease joy; when the month of *Adar* begins, we increase joy. (*Ta'anit* 29a)

There is a rabbinic directive to increase our happiness in the Jewish month of *Adar* and to decrease our happiness in the Jewish month of *Av*. This instruction is meant to bring attention to the fact that we are entering a time of redemption and salvation beginning with the Hebrew month of *Adar*, in which the holiday of Purim occurs (and that period continues straight through to the holiday of Pesach

[Passover], which celebrates the Exodus from Egypt). This time period lies in direct contrast with the arrival of the Hebrew month of *Av*, which commemorates the cessation of the sacrifices in, and destruction of, the Temples. And yet the rabbinic dictum makes a correlation between these two diametrically opposite times. Just as in *Av* we decrease, so too in *Adar* we increase. These diametrically opposite months share one thing in common: *simchah*. Regardless of the nature of the event, from the most miraculous to the most devastating, a person, dare I say, can always be in a state of *simchah*, whether it be elevated or muted. Mourning and celebrating, destroying and rebuilding, and everything in between, must always be done and *can* always be done with *simchah*.

> For in joy shall you come forth.   (Isaiah 55:12)

The *simchah* cannot refer to what is described in the vernacular as "happiness" or even "joy." The presence of *simchah* is not just an emotion but also the cognizance of a deep sense of purpose, equanimity and fulfillment. Surely there are elements of joy and even possibly some levity manifested in this attitude. But what is abundantly clear is that this is not some sort of transient state like other emotions. It's not a fleeting burst of laughter or merriment – a "rush" that accompanies a particular experience. It is something much deeper than that, something that is much more profound and true. Life is filled with emotions and their ephemeral nature, but *simchah* can always be your anchor. Even if you are in the grip of so called "negative" emotions, the feelings of sadness and despair, you can still feel a sense of well-being around that sadness. "We decrease" – diminish oneself – but with *simchah*. Similarly, even when you are in the waves of ecstasy, you maintain your *simchah* as well. "We increase" – expansiveness and growth – all the while contained by the vessel of *simchah*. Therefore, the prerequisite for *simchah* does not require us to be giddy or happy all the time, making painful and difficult emotions taboo. That negates rather than reinforces our humanity. It would be troubling and even pathological if a person broke into song on hearing news of a tragedy or illness. These emotions are also Divinely inspired, with each one, regardless of association be it positive or negative, vital for our growth, maturity and wellbeing.

Simchah is not about putting a superficial, shiny, happy face on things, or refusing to acknowledge the hard things in life. It is about dwelling in joy. Willingly accepting the will of God and our role in a divine plan. Not being happy, but having *simchah,* experiencing everything we encounter in life as contained within this vast vessel called *simchah.* It is about a steady, unremitting sense of well-being that is a place of refuge a person can always call home. *Simchah* becomes the receptacle for the experiences of our lives, the frame that holds them, the space they go through. The refuge of *simchah* will remove a person from constricted consciousness into a redeemed state of being.

As long as resentment and feelings of unworthiness dominate, one is in a personal state of exile. This feeling of alienation isn't just felt by the individual. These feelings are shared with God who we are told "suffers" as well. The capacity to experience the Divine Presence in one's life directly corresponds to the presence of *simchah* in a person's heart. *Simchah* is an acknowledgement of God's presence infused in the present. The exile of the heart, of the *Shechinah* and of the Jewish people are all one and the same. God suffers with us while we are in exile. The deepest pain of the Divine Presence being in exile is caused when the Jewish heart is overwhelmed with sadness, as the verse states, "[God] became grieved in His heart" (Genesis 6:6). "He shall call upon Me, and I will answer him; I will be *with* him in his misfortune" (Psalms 91:16). The ability to sense Divinity, Godliness, in everything – most importantly, in one's self – corresponds directly to the *simchah* in one's heart. When a person is not in a state of *simchah*, his ability to have *yishuv hada'at* is inherently obscured.

Therefore, when the prophet Isaiah describes the redemption, he states, "You shall depart the exile with joy" (Isaiah 55:12). The simple meaning of this statement is that when you leave the exile, you will be happy. The emotion accompanying your redemption will be *simchah.* However, on a deeper level, the verse is teaching us the key to redemption. Only through cultivating and living with *simchah* can a person ever truly leave exile. It is causative. If exile is the sadness, then *simchah is* the redemption. If exile is the symptom, *simchah* is the cure. Once a person is living *b'simchah* he is free.

From the very beginning of the Jewish people, the main desire of the children of Abraham has been for the redemption and ability to abide in the *simchah* that is ever-present in their lives. Our deep longing for *simchah* is the concurrent longing for redemption. Falling into sadness is falling into exile, while cultivating and dwelling in *simchah* is redemption. The first command God said to Abram (not yet Abraham) was the directive, *Lech lecha*. God's call to Abraham and to all of his descendants is, "Go [into] yourself from your land, birthplace and your father's home to the land that I will show you. And there you will find blessing" (Genesis 12:1–2).

In the Kabbalistic works, we are taught that Abram is the soul that has not yet uncovered the letter *hey* that has the numerical value in Hebrew numerology of five. That *hey*, the last letter of the name *Yud-Hey-Vav* and *Hey*, represents the five sounds of joy that the prophet Jeremiah spoke of in his prophecy of redemption (Jeremiah 33:11).

The Kabbalistic works, when describing the Jewish soul in its saddened state, refers to it as Abram, without the letter *hey*. To become Abraham, which is the fulfillment of the soul's deepest longing to fully actualize itself with these five sounds of joy, marked the beginning of the path of the Jewish people in the world. The goal of Abram and all his future descendants is to be transformed into Abraham, to be filled with the letter *hey*, the five expressions of joy.

Therefore, God tells Abraham, "If you want to find *simchah*, you must go into yourself. *Simchah* happens only in the present moment, and in each and every present moment. It is now, and now, and now. . . . The miracle and mystery of your life is accessible only here and now. But not only that, in order to become Abraham you must go into yourself from your land. You must go into where and who you are, to fully connect to the physical place you are in – not to be attached to physical life but to be fully present to what you have, without needing or striving for more.

Our natural inclination towards sadness as human beings results from being too attached to the physical world. Psychologists have demonstrated a negativity bias that colors and shades all aspects of our lives. One bad experience can wipe out the pleasure of a thousand positive previous ones. When we look back at our day or even our life, what memories and events tend to stand out more: the successes or the failures, the triumphs or the defeats? When physical life doesn't work out perfectly well, a person can be buried in sadness. We dwell on our own inadequacies and our sufferings, resenting their intrusion to the point that we forget our own blessings.

If your *simchah* depends totally on this physical world, you are doomed to a life of suffering. God therefore tells Abram that to achieve *simchah* he must connect fully with the physical place he is in at each and every moment. Therein lies true *simchah*.

However, it is not enough for a person to connect to the physical place he is in. He must also go into the place of his birth and the house of his father. Some people believe that happiness and holiness depend solely on their childhood experiences and upbringing, and that the nature of a child's genetic background and surroundings will dictate with minimal opportunity for deviation, all future possibility of happiness.

Additionally, the cultural milieu in which a person is brought up pales in comparison to the difficulty of experiencing *simchah* based on the experiences of his parent's home. As much as you love your parents and as much as your parents might love you, there can be an undetectable sadness, angst, dissatisfaction and frustration cultivated by the opinions and pressure that a person finds in his or her home. The one place where a person nurtures expectations of unconditional peace and love, can often also be the headquarters of terrible misunderstandings accompanied by terrible amounts of pain.

Growing up in the conditions of "your father's house," even with – and often in spite of – all the love, is almost inevitably accompanied by difficulties associated with "your father's house." One does not need a PhD in psychology to recognize the truth of this last statement. God tells Abram, "If you want to become Abraham, you must go into every aspect of yourself." You must understand what influenced you, so you can independently evaluate, accept, refine, reject, adapt, and internalize, as appropriate to you. In order to experience *simchah*, a person has to become his own person, regardless of childhood experiences.

This of course is not an admonition to disassociate from one's past. God's instruction is just the opposite. In order for Abram to uncover the letter *hey* latent in his life, he must "go into" his parents' home. He must accept things as they are. He must accept the difficulties and challenges that his home life presented for him. In order to find himself and transcend the sadness that comes from not yet being who he is destined to become, he must completely accept all the pieces of his life. There is nothing in his life to disavow or sublimate. Once Abram can fully accept and integrate his past, then and only then can he go to "the land that I will show you." Only then can he enter the source and land of *simchah*, the Promised Land of Israel.

When Abraham uncovered the letter *hey* and found *simchah* in all facets of his life, he demonstrated for each of his children how to achieve *simchah*. By not disavowing but rather by going into himself – into his physical nature, his upbringing and all of his family baggage – he could uncover the vessel of joy. His personal journey constitutes the road map for all of his descendants to be redeemed from their personal exile through the path of *simchah*.

A Reflection on Joy

The Talmud tells the story of Rabbi Beroka, who stood with Elijah the prophet in the market and asked him, "Is there anyone here who belongs in the World to Come?" Elijah pointed out two brothers. So Rabbi Beroka ran after the two brothers and asked them what their business was. They replied, "We are jesters. We make depressed people laugh. And when we see two people in a quarrel, we use some humor to make peace between them." The Baal Shem Tov asked heaven for an explanation of this, and this is what he was told in a vision:

These two jesters were able to connect every matter they saw in a person to its origin in the higher world. By doing this, any harsh heavenly decrees upon this person were automatically annulled. But if someone was depressed, they could not make this connection. So they would cheer him up with some humorous words, until they were able to make all the connections necessary. (*Keter Shem Tov* 272)

The main reason why people are far from God is because their minds are not settled and they do not pause to consider the purpose of their existence. But when a person is happy, his mind becomes settled and he is able to understand things clearly. Someone who is anxious and depressed finds it impossible to direct his thoughts where he wants. It is hard for him to calm and settle his mind. Only when a person is happy can he direct his thoughts wherever he wants and settle his mind.

Joy is the world of freedom – "for you shall go out with joy." (Isaiah 55:12) Through joy we become free and leave our exile. When a person maintains a happy, joyous attitude, his mind and thoughts become free and he is no longer in exile. He can then direct his thoughts as he wants and settle his mind so as to focus on his goal and draw close to God.

(*Likutey Moharan* II, 10)

Hamtein: Patience

THE MESSAGE OF *LECH LECHA* incorporates the attitude of always trying to get somewhere. We move toward something better or at least something different than what is happening right now. *Lech Lecha* suggests an implicit direction from God that there must be something better than what is happening right now: a better time, a better job, a better anything else. That inevitably leads to a concomitant need for some certainty to respond to the question of when will it all finally come together? From the back seat, asks the child, are we there yet? Very often, this almost visceral need to get somewhere, anywhere, rather than be right here, causes us to become driven, impatient, and frustrated.

What often follows are words we wish we could take back, decisions we regret and actions that often fly directly in the face of the values we espouse. Are we condemned to be constantly in motion? Or is there some respite?

"Have you seen the man who is hasty? There is more hope for the fool than for him" (Proverbs 29:20). A person who acts in haste isn't just being rash and foolhardy. In fact, he might be very intelligent, seeking answers whose time for revelation has not yet come. He is simply living without *yishuv hada'at*, like a child who, unable to wait for the butterfly to emerge from the cocoon on its own, prematurely peels it apart. Unfortunately for him (and even more unfortunately for that butterfly), his haste denotes a lack of understanding of the nature of things – that they must unfold in their own time.

> And you shall perish hastily from off the good land which the Lord gives to you. (Deuteronomy 11:17)

The literal interpretation of this verse is fairly evident, but the Baal Shem Tov explained it as a transitive, to mean that a person needs to actively eliminate the quality of rushing. What needs to perish? The attitude of haste. Haste is the trait of endless doing, of getting things done in a hurried rush that is the external manifestation of a mind and soul in a state of unease.

One of the fundamental attitudinal qualities required for the cultivation of *yishuv hada'at* is to pay attention to one's need to rush and get through everything. A person must allow himself to approach whatever he is doing with focus. The need to "finish it up" or "just get it over with" is completely antithetical to this. Such physical activity done without *yishuv hada'at* will more often than not result in something inevitably going wrong (such as the number of emergency-room visits on a Sunday due to the distracted attention span of people cutting bagels). It stands to reason that in the spiritual, psychological realm, this will certainly be true as well. An attitude of "Am I there yet?" or "Can't we hurry this up already?" will do nothing to calm a person's torrent of unruly thoughts. So if a person is caught up in a frenzy of rushing (and isn't everyone caught up in that to some extent?), the chances of cultivating mindful presence are slim to none.

This is a non-negotiable starting point. If a person wants to look at his life through the prism of *yishuv hada'at* and experience life as it is without being swept away by thoughts and feelings, then this must be the first step of the process. A person simply cannot get started unless he makes a commitment to slow things down to the speed at which they are actually happening. "*Hamtein,*" (Wait) was something that Rebbe Nachman of Breslov would often tell his students. Because what is happening right now is exactly what is supposed to be happening. Not what you think should be happening and not something you can force to occur.

Underlying this is an imperative to cease trying to force things to happen, but rather, to allow things to be as they are. The attitude of "perish hastily" means that not only must a person extinguish the need to see automatic results, but he must commit himself with deep trust to the sense that things are as they should be. With that intention, with that first commitment, he already begins to feel the sense of peace brought by *yishuv hada'at* because he is accepting reality. Nothing has been accomplished other than allowing things to take place at the pace that they are actually happening. Rushing and self-imposed deadlines will never allow a person to just be with his thoughts, to just experience his emotions and see them exactly as they are. Only then can meaningful actions take place. If you are stuck in the role of the person referred to in Jewish ethical works as experiencing *bihilut* (which really doesn't have an accurate translation but conjures up the image of the Tasmanian devil, a frenzied whirlwind of aimless activity), the grim result is inevitably that this whirlwind of activity leaves absolute devastation in its wake. Sadly, that is an accurate description of our day-to-day lives.

As noted above, this rushing to accomplish meaningful goals is likely to result in more harm than good. A person might be getting a lot of things done, and he may think it is his natural inclination to go through things quickly, but the "gain is offset by the loss" (*Pirkei Avot* 5:11). The need to achieve and accomplish and the desire to be done with something prevents a person from ever truly attaining this state of presence, which ironically is the real purpose of all of these stratagems and urgency. There *is* more hope for a fool than for him!

> Torah leads to watchfulness; Watchfulness leads to Zeal.
> (*Avodah Zara* 20b)

Cultivating an attitude of *hamtein* does not contradict another fundamental trait in Jewish spiritual development, the attitude of *zrizut* (alacrity and zeal). One should not mistakenly assume that this trait demands moving briskly with arms and legs flailing in quick succession to maximize the amount one can accomplish during the day. In the Jewish ethical books, the attitude of *zrizut* always follows the cultivation of the attribute of *zehirut* (watchfulness). That means before a person acts in any endeavor or task, he must carefully make a conscientious choice, what to do and what not to do. He is watchful, careful to keep the focus on the task at hand without allowing distractions, either external or internal, to obscure his focus from his chosen goal. A person who is acting with *zrizut* isn't a person who is speeding through his chores and checking items off his to-do list at a breakneck pace. He is deliberate, calculated and able to accomplish what he sets out to do without distraction. He has evaluated the situation and determined the appropriate goal and methodology for achieving it. This is the zeal that the Torah praises. This can only be acquired when one is watchful, when one has learned how to live with *hamtein*. The combination of *hamtein, zehirut,* and *zrizut* leads to purposeful, efficient, and effective action.

The entire world is overwhelmed with the need to do things faster. Ironically, all of the technological advances meant to increase our leisure and life satisfaction have created the opposite result. The "need for speed" results in an almost automatic reaction of disgust if a website takes more than a fraction of a second to load or a page more than a few seconds to print. Annoyance, frustration, upgrades . . . leading to more annoyance, frustration, upgrades. The whole nature of our world has devolved into a sense of being harried, and this attitude affects all areas of our lives. Instant gratification or nothing. One thing is certain: if a person hasn't developed this attitude that he must "perish" the "haste" that is driving him, then he is surely suffering from the anxiety that the impulse to be hasty engenders. In the realm of cultivating real peace of mind, where a person thinks he has internalized some of the true secrets of life, wanting things to be accomplished in a hasty manner stands diametrically opposed to real and honest, in-depth growth. If a person feels compelled to be finished very quickly, and not take the time to allow things to take their natural course, his gains, while admirable, will inevitably be for naught.

Even more than this trait being a necessity for personal growth, the individual who has cultivated the attitude of "*hamtein*" is able to see the Divine aspects latent within the waiting as well. The Talmud teaches that if a person seeks to defile himself by sinning, the path lies open before him. Conversely, "One who comes to purify himself receives assistance from above" (*Yoma* 38b). To illustrate this, they provide the parable of a merchant who sells both kerosene and perfume. When someone enters the store to buy kerosene, the store owner who is busy in the back storeroom, not wanting to get his hands dirty, can't be bothered and tells the person to measure it himself. However, when a different customer walks in wanting to buy the most aromatic expensive perfume in the store, the owner calls out, "Wait and I will measure it out for you in order that we can both enjoy it together." God waits with you. He knows how badly you want to get "there" but first there is a special requirement that has to be fulfilled. You must define and understand the "there." You must chart the best route to get "there." And perhaps most important, you must wait for the right time. Only then, by internalizing that understanding throughout the waiting process, will you benefit from the good latent within the process of "*hamtein*" as well.

If you truly want to cultivate *yishuv hada'at*, to be a person who will no longer be hijacked by his feelings, desires and thoughts, and be able to channel all of your thoughts and feelings in the valued direction of your life, you must have the attitude of accepting the gradual nature of things. Be prepared to cultivate this carefully and most importantly, patiently. Shift from the mindset of rushing, to an attitude of *hamtein* – "waiting." This is the key to all beginnings: to look carefully and see clearly what truly is right now. Anything else is only self-delusion. "Wait and both of us will be able to enjoy it together." (*Yoma* 38b)

A Reflection on Patience

When you just can't fall asleep, it's no use trying to force yourself to sleep. The more you try to force yourself, the more will sleep elude you. The same applies to many other things: it is not good to force yourself too much, because the more you try to force yourself, the stronger the opposing forces will become.

At times this applies even to prayer and devotion. You should certainly make every possible effort to sanctify yourself and attain true devotion. When something can be done today, don't leave it for tomorrow, because the world never stops for a moment. Man's world consists only of the present. Whatever you can do to serve God, do immediately and determinedly without delay. Who knows what obstacles you may face from the outside and from within if you leave it until later?

But at times you may see that, despite all your efforts and determination, you simply cannot achieve what you want. Sometimes you must simply wait. Don't be discouraged because you are not achieving what you want. Don't let this push you off course. You must wait a little until the time is ripe.

The most important thing of all is to look to God at all times with longing and yearning, even when things are not going as well as you would like in your prayers and devotions. Never despair, no matter what. And as soon as God gives you the opportunity to do something holy, do it at once.

(Chayey Moharan #431)

Sod: Living a Secret Life

THERE ARE A LOT OF BOOKS that have the word "secret" in the title – over 80,000 in the Kindle store alone! Presumably, the prevailing wisdom behind this is that books that have the word "secret" in the title have an increased chance of selling. It seems that everybody wants to know the secret of whatever it is that has been eluding him or her up until this point in their lives. If we only knew the secret, we could be . . . thin, smart, rich, funny – you name it. Based on the patients I see, I am fairly certain that I am not the only person walking around who must contend with a general sense of dissatisfaction with my life. There appears to be a constant, faint, but pervasive feeling that something is just not quite right, and that precipitates an urge to quell or silence this feeling immediately. And if someone has a secret to somehow dispel these feelings and thoughts, then I (and, apparently, millions of Kindle customers) will gladly pay $14.95 to know it. Now if you were to ask your average fairly educated Jew armed with a traditional Jewish background, where the secrets of the Torah – the books of *sod* (which means "secret" in Hebrew) – are to be found, the answer would invariably be "in the Kabbalah," the Jewish mystical works. Just as people jump to books with the word "secret" in the title, some leap to these mystical works for an antidote to quiet the anxieties in their lives. These works include, but are not limited to, the Zohar, and the writings of the Ari (Rabbi Yitzchak Luria) and his students. These are what are commonly referred to as the works containing the secrets of Torah, the books of *sod.*

Jewish wisdom teaches that there are two types of secrets. There is the secret that hides wonderful news. Maybe you just found out that you will be getting a new promotion, or a couple discovers that they are expecting a child. These people withhold these wonderful tidings, biding their time, waiting for the right time to share them with the whole world; not right now, but when the right time comes, they will be able to reveal this secret to everyone. They are deferring disclosure until the exact moment when the timing is right. "Oh, you'll know soon enough," they might remark with a knowing smile.

However, as secretive as they may be, that's not a real secret. Any secret that a person can tell, even if he takes it to his grave and never reveals it, does not qualify in the Jewish wisdom as *sod*. True, it's something that he hasn't shared, and it might be something that he will never ever share with another living soul, but the possibility that it can be told, that a person could decide to share, means that it's not really a secret. Accordingly, even the mystical works of kabbalah and the Zohar are not *sod*. As deep and as complicated as they are, these are not called the secrets of Torah. If there is a kabbalah center with whatever it is selling popping up on the corner of your block, how secretive can it really be? It's not as if these books are hard to come by. And if a person is blessed with the ability to read, then he can open up these books and peruse them at his leisure. They are no more secret than the works of Shakespeare, available to all (even if they are accessible and comprehensible only to the educated few). That is not the secret Torah.

While these works are very difficult to comprehend, and their terminology is archaic and complex, written in a manner intended to obfuscate their meanings to the uninitiated, nonetheless, that still doesn't qualify them as secret. Is a menu written in Chinese a secret just because you are unable to comprehend it? How about the indecipherable quantum physics book you just picked up – would that qualify? Just because you don't speak the language or understand the concepts does not transform the material into a secret. It's open and revealed for anyone who can speak the language and understand the material. And it is most definitely not *sod*.

What is a real secret, then? What is the attitude of *sod* that we are tasked to cultivate in order to attain *yishuv hada'at*? One of the cardinal sins of a therapist is to tell a client that he understands what they are going through. More often than not, that statement will be met with incredulousness or, more likely, righteous indignation. That response stems from the simple truth that one can never presume to truly "understand" another person. Empathize? Of course!

Categorize on the basis of vast experience? Yes. But understand? Even in regard to a shared experience, their understanding remains exclusive to them and them alone, because each of them is unique.

A secret is something that people can talk about, post on the Internet, and share on every social media platform, without changing its status as a secret. A person can write about it using rivers of ink, and still no one could reveal it, because the essence is a secret. Try to describe the taste of your mother's chocolate chip cookies to someone who has never once had a cookie. Colors will remain secrets from the blind, and symphonies from the deaf. That taste, sight, and sound is something that is beyond any words that can be communicated to another person who hasn't experienced it. While not hidden, these secrets cannot be shared, because they are unique to a person's experience and sensibility.

No matter how many times you repeat the words, "I love you," no matter how hard you try to find the exact phrase to describe the emotion, you will inevitably come up short, for, while it definitely exists and can be deeply felt, no description can suffice – that love you have for another person remains a secret, a *sod*. Even if the people at Hallmark were somehow able to transcribe what you want to express, it would make no difference, because even after the card was delivered and the secret let out, it would still invariably remain a secret. The *sod* has not been violated. My description of how much I love my child are words that every person can read but cannot understand, because a secret in its essence can never be fully conveyed. Words are the most powerful way of trying to transmit thoughts and feelings. But they are just garments. The essence remains as secret as it ever was, just as before a person talked about it.

So *sod* is not just reserved for kabbalah. *Sod* is everything in life. A person may have authored the most authoritative book on parenting techniques, but no matter how voluminous a work it is, it pales in comparison to the actual experience of parenting. All the child-rearing books in the world cannot compare to the *sod* when the author has her own child. All the tomes composed on the subject of love, the sonnets and songs composed in its name, are nothing remotely close to being in love. It's not a case of apples and oranges, but of apples and a different species entirely. It's revealed vs. secret. It is no longer just talking about, but being.

A real secret is something that's impossible to explain, define and share. It is found within the person and cannot be revealed to anyone. *Sod* is a person's inner way of feeling something, sensing something that simply isn't accessible to anyone else. You can teach and learn something your brain can understand, be it physics, Chinese or esoteric kabbalah. You can read whatever you want. But a *sod* cannot be taught, because it is how your soul grasps something. It's no longer a body of knowledge, separate and discrete from your own identity, where there is you and the notion of whatever concept you are contemplating, discussing, or writing about. No longer are you a person writing about love, parenting or this moment. Rather, the subject is subsumed in you.

Similarly, a person can write many books on the subject of God, or give countless speeches about God, and even pray daily, yet he and God are two separate realities. He has never "tasted" God in the moment. He can be brilliant and eloquent and published, while the truth remains that he is not connected at all. How can that connection be actualized? Through attachment to the present – the same way a researcher into parenting, who knows every available relevant statistic, can become one with being a parent only by becoming a parent (which until this time in his life remained a theoretical idea and concept). Only through fully connecting to the now can one attach himself to God, and finally stop talking to, at, and about God and be *with* Him.

> Speak unto the children of Israel, saying: If any man of you or of your generations shall be unclean by reason of a dead body, or be in a journey afar off, yet he shall keep the Passover unto the Lord.   (Numbers 9:10)

The moment a secret is revealed or shared it ceases to be a secret. But a true *sod* is different entirely. It's a *sod* of how you grasp something from within yourself, from the place where you are standing. There is a remarkable interpretation given by one of the great Hasidic masters regarding the law of the second paschal offering. The verse allows for a makeup to those who for various reasons could not partake in the offering the first time around. If a person is ritually impure or finds himself at a great distance from the Temple in Jerusalem, he is absolved of the requirement to bring the offering and is provided with this dispensation for a makeup opportunity. Rashi (the foremost medieval commentator on the Torah) explains, based on the sages, that "a great distance" means that even if he is a foot outside the Temple Mount he is considered absolved due to this exemption. Even if he was standing on the threshold of the Temple Mount, mere inches away, this would still be called a distant journey.

From a practical standpoint, this is extremely puzzling. How can a minor distance of a few feet, even a few inches, be considered enough to absolve a person of his obligation? However, recall that distance in spirituality is not a matter of physical proximity. This person may physically be adjacent to where he needs to be, but yet be too distant to participate. This distance is in his soul. If a person feels far away from God, to the point where, when he recites a blessing with the formula "Blessed are You" he is unable to articulate it with the warmth, affection and certainty of how he would speak to his closest and most dear friend, face-to-face, then that too places him in the parameters of being far away. Physically he might be five inches away from where he needs to be, but he is still standing on the outside looking in, far away.

If a person doesn't feel God in his mind, body and soul that right here in the place where he is right now when he says the words "Blessed are You," then he is considered to be outside the prescribed place. Jewish law considers him to be in the category of being far away. Regardless of the Torah knowledge that he may have accrued and the religious comprehension for which he has become a repository, he has never once tasted the secret. It's all outside, in the revealed world. He is not in Jerusalem. He is not in the Temple. He is not in the holy of holies.

Say and feel the presence of the word "You." If you can't say "You" when speaking to God, like a person speaking to his dearest, most intimate friend, you are outside. You are not in the world of *sod*. But when a person says "You" with the sublime sense of all that the relationship entails – the indescribable feeling of presence, the ineffable feeling of the now – he has entered the world of *sod*.

> Take your shoes off your feet, because the place upon which you stand is holy soil.　　　　　　　　　　(Exodus 3:5)

When a person shifts from a mindset of learning and studying about God to cultivating being in the felt presence of God, it becomes crystal clear to him (and not in an intellectual sense) that He is present, filling this very moment. He exists, and there is no one else in the world with whom this person can share that secret, the secret he has uncovered within himself. That *yishuv hada'at* becomes a revealed, living, simple reality: God is with me; I am with God. God cares about me. God has a vested interest in me. All this time he has experienced life like the researcher writing about parenting or the poet composing sonnets about love. When they experience being a parent or falling in love, that experience takes them to the world of *sod* with respect to these emotions.

To live the secret of life and not just the external trappings, to unite with God, a person needs to recognize that the place where he is standing, is the holy of holies. And in that place he is able to enact a unification that is beyond what any mystical lecture could provide. The real secret is that everything is built upon and is flowing from attachment to the Creator, attachment that can only happen in the moment. A person who lives with a constant awareness that the place where he stands is also the place where God is to be found is living with the secret of creation, that the Divine is here with us, present and available.

> For I know that the Lord is great.   (Psalms 135:5)

We are all standing in a secret. A person can learn the deepest mysteries of the Torah and remain on the outside. A person can learn about the highest Kabbalistic spheres or read about the connection that this moment provides, but he is still far, far away.

But if he is completely immersed in that moment, in that verse, in that law, in that feeling, in that place, then at that moment he is connected to the secret of Torah. King David was precise in his usage of the word "I know" (as opposed to "I believe"), because only he knew precisely at that moment what he was feeling; knowledge that could never be relayed to or shared with anyone else. "I can't tell you but I know it." This crystallizes the difference between talking about vs. being with God. "I know the secret." It is the message of living a life that's no longer "a far off voyage" consisting of just talking about God, or living a superficial life, in which a person is unable honestly to say "You." The whole purpose of living is to attach oneself to God. The secrets of Torah are understood by those who attach completely to the moment in which they find themselves, where even in the most banal of instances, one can feel every single cell in his body come alive with the presence found in this moment.

> For there the Lord has commanded blessing, life unto eternity. (Psalms 133:3)

"There." This is where blessing is to be found. This is where true life is to be experienced. It's no longer a concept or theorem or antiquated belief, but rather a revitalizing reality breathing existence into every moment. And you must be there. Because once you are there, when you complete the moment, then you are fully living, eternally. Attachment to the now is to be in love and not just to write about it, but to be present to it and not to intellectualize about it. "There" is the Temple and Jerusalem and this moment. It's the place of life. It is the opposite of separation, in which a person is standing outside on a "distant" journey. Because as soon as a person can live with the felt existence of "Blessed are You," like a person speaking to his dearest friend face-to-face, he is living his secret, accessible to no one but himself and God. To feel that connection to the place where one is standing – that is living with the secret of the Torah.

> Fortunate are those who understand your secrets.
> (*Piyut Bar Yochai*)

A Reflection on the Place of God

We learn in the holy book *Beit-Aharon* that the fact that God gave the Torah to the Jewish people in the wilderness was of great significance. The *Beit-Aharon's* teaching is in reference to Rashi's explanation of the verse (Deut. 6:5) "You must love God your Lord with all your heart." Rashi (ibid.) explains: "Your heart should not be divided against God." The Hebrew name for God used in this Rashi is *HaMakom*, which in this context is translated as "Omnipresent," but normally translates as "Place." The *Beit Aharon* explains Rashi as saying, "Your heart should not be divided against the place." That we must never say, "In this place I can worship God, but in another place it would not be possible." Wherever we are, we must worship God. If the Jewish people had received the Torah in their own land, the Land of Israel, they might have assumed that they could fulfill the commandments only in their own homes, and not when they were exiled and preoccupied with survival. This is why God gave them the Torah in the wilderness, while they were traveling and busy – so that they would know to keep the Torah everywhere, as we said above, "that your heart should not be divided against the place."

Aish Kodesh, Parshat Yitro s.v. *Vayishma Yitro*

A Yiddish Song by Rabbi Levi Yitzchak of Berditchev

Riboyno shel oylom,	Master of the Universe!
Ich vil dir a dudele shpilen:	I will sing a song to You (familiar).
Riboyno shel oylom, Ich vil dir a	Where shall I seek You, Master of
dudele zingen:	the Universe?
Onoh emtzoekho, Riboyno shel oylom?	And where shall I not seek You,
V'onoh lo emtzoekho, Riboyno shel	Master of the Universe?
oylom?	Where can I find You, Master of
Avu kon ich dir gefinen, Riboyno shel	the Universe?
oylom?	And where can I not find You,
Un avu zol ich dir nit gefinen,	Master of the Universe?
Riboyno shel oylom?	
Az mailoh du, matoh du,	You, above; You, below;
mizroch du,mayrov du, dorem du,	East, You; West, You;
tzofen du.	South, You; North, You.
Du du, du du, DU!!	You . . . You!
du du du, du du, du, du du du, du	You. You. You. You.
du du	
Az iz gut iz doch du, choliloh nit oich du	When things are good, You.
un az du iz doch gut.	Heaven forbid, when they are not
Du du, du du, DU!!	good, also You.
du du du, du du, du, du du du, du	You . . . You! You. You. You. You.
du du	
Mailoh du, matoh du	
mizroch du, mayrov du, dorem du,	
tzofen du,	
DU DU!!	
Mailoh du, matoh du	
mizroch du, mayrov du,	
du du, du du, du du du, du du du	
ay ay ay ay. . . .	
Mailoh du, matoh du,	
mizroch du, mayrov du, dorem du,	
tzofen du,	
Du, du, DU!!	
du du du, du, du, DU DU DU!!!	
DU DU DU!	

Meniot: Obstacles

H
OW DID ABRAHAM KNOW?" asked my cab
driver out of the blue. Cab drivers in Israel are the un-
official experts on every topic, ranging from politics to
religion and everything in between. One of the perks of living in
Israel is that whether or not you asked for it, you are going to get
random advice, encouragement and chastisement from pretty much
everyone you meet on the street. It is almost part of the national
ethos that if you are there, they are going to share their opinion with
you. And they aren't the least bit shy about doing it.

I had learned from previous experiences that my cab driver must
already know the answer to his question but expected me to play
along. I asked, "How did he know what?"

"How did Abraham know that the ram that was caught in the
brambles wasn't some ploy of Satan to dupe him?" he replied. He
was referring of course to the binding of Isaac, when, at the moment that Abraham was about to fulfill the puzzling divine decree to
slaughter his precious son, God commanded Abraham to cease and
desist and instead raise his eyes to where he saw a ram caught in the
thicket to serve as a substitute. I said, "I'm not really sure."

He then turned around (still driving, of course) and said, "Because
he had to work for it, he still had to untangle the ram from the
thicket. Had it been just there waiting for him in plain sight, he
would have to suspect it was some sort of ruse." I thanked him for
the insight, but was happier that he had turned back to face the road
again.

The more I thought about it afterwards, the more I wondered if
it were true. I mean, clearly, this isn't always the case, right? The best
things in life are free! When God gives us something, it doesn't always

come with a challenge or struggle. But his words got me thinking about the question of "Where was God when . . . ?" Unfortunately, there is no end to questions and disasters with which a person can fill in the blank. Has the thought, "If I were God, I certainly wouldn't have allowed X or Y to happen," ever occurred to you? It certainly has raced through my mind more than once or twice. I sometimes engage in a very unproductive daydreaming exercise that consists of imagining things I'd do differently if I were God. If I am not careful, this game can go on for quite some time.

But the truth is that if we knew the answers to, for example, why the righteous suffer and the evil prosper, we would be running the show. But that is the point about God: He is unknowable, at least in the way that we would define "knowing." It's one of the things that makes Him God, and us not-God. That doesn't mean that there can't be a real, intimate connection between us, and that we shouldn't try to understand His ways. Of course, attaining that requires knowing how to look.

We are taught from an early age that life is far from simple, but there is still some part of us that resists this reality and we keep coming up against this question of "Why does it have to be so hard for me?" We all have our questions. And these questions become complications, tribulations and obstacles. These questions become the *meniot* in our lives.

What exactly are *meniot*? *Meniot* are the hindrances – imagined and real, physical and spiritual – that seem to stand in the way of our getting to where we want our journey to take us, impediments that make the possibility of *yishuv hada'at* seem near impossible.

"Look who suddenly wants to turn things around!" whispers the voice in your head. "Can you believe it? All of a sudden, you want to stop drinking, lose twenty pounds, stop yelling at your kids, commit to a life of devotion, good deeds, and meaning. How successful have you been in the past?" I am fairly certain that I am not the only one who sometimes thinks and feels this way. Any time a person feels that he wants to do the right thing, instantaneously a counterargument stands up and opposes it. This adversarial judgment – which may come from the outside but far more often comes from within – does not support him when he wishes to proceed on the path of valued living.

As a result of these judgmental thoughts, an obstruction has been placed squarely on this path of growth and change. These are the *meniot* of our lives. They can be formed from thoughts, words and deeds, all of which join together to form impediments. Ultimately, these doubts and criticizing states of mind become the obstacles to all growth and development.

Anyone who has come into my office looking to change his or her life can attest to this reality. But I needn't look further than my own life experiences to know that this struggle is very real. If you haven't experienced these obstacles, it simply means that you haven't tried to change. If you have *tried* to change, if you have *tried* to progress, if you have *tried* to flourish, you know that sooner or later, most likely sooner, these obstructions will be sure to arise. You respond to external forces in your life, but it is internal resistance that blocks the path to progress. These *meniot* operate within everyone. Their presence is not indicative of a personal failing or flaw. However, as ubiquitous as these *meniot* are, our gut reaction is to avoid them at all cost. We have been taught from a young age that pain and suffering are to be avoided. And for the most part, that is true.

But at what cost? What if these *meniot* are not merely road blocks, but devices to facilitate personal growth and development? What if they are not merely a good opportunity to learn something about internal resources and to bolster character development in the way of "whatever does not kill me only makes me stronger"? What if this resistance served a greater purpose? What if a person cannot fully be who he is until he has learned how to relate to his *meniot*? How can he learn that precisely during these encounters with painful *meniot* there exists the possibility to connect himself to something beyond himself?

When Menachem Mendel of Kotzk was a young boy, he began to develop a reputation for being a prodigy with a sharp wit. One of the townspeople thought he might trip him up with a sly question. "Mendel," he said, "I will give you a gold coin if you can show me where God is." Young Mendel, not even looking up from his studies, responded, "And I will give you two if you tell me where He is not."

What would you answer if someone asked you, "Where is God?" Would you point to the sky? Respond that He is everywhere? Maybe in Jerusalem? In the synagogue, perhaps?

The Talmud says that the answer a person should give if someone asks him, "Where is your God?" is "God resides in the great metropolis of Rome."

"Where is your God?" Funny you should ask. Ironically, the last place you would think to find God is exactly where the Talmud suggests you can find Him. In rabbinic literature, Rome is the epitome of Godlessness. Rome is the abode of the descendants of Esau, Jacob's adversary, the twin brother who abandons the way of Abraham and Isaac and stands for unbridled appetite and physicality. Rome is the destroyer of God's Temple, and yet, ironically, according to the Talmud, it is apparently God's address as well. Rome, whose entire existence serves as the paradigm antithetical to the revelation of God's existence in the world, doubles as God's forwarding address.

And in truth, who is this questioner to whom the Talmud refers? Of course, the Talmud isn't referring to a bystander on the street who is asking for directions. The person to whom the Talmud refers is someone who is encountering tremendous difficulties in his life, in the form of the most intimidating, complex and horrible of obstacles. The questioner is none other than the person himself! (Because when the going gets tough, the questions get tougher.) "Where is your God?" This is the most oppressive *meniah* of all. "Where is your God? Where is your God right now?" "Where is God when I need Him most of all?" The Talmud replies that the answer to this question is that He is in the city of Rome. "He is calling to me from Rome," says the prophet Isaiah. (Isaiah 21:11)

The answer to this question is that God is in the last place in the world that a person would think to search for and find Him: Rome, the antithesis of holiness, the headquarters of impurity, the darkest darkness of all. (The Talmud also relates that Rome is where the Messiah is waiting, because that will also be the source of a person's redemption.) Rome is a person's realization that he has sunken to the lowest place and he does not know how to get out. And just as a person is trying to climb out, he finds that all of the filth of Rome is blocking and overwhelming him.

"Where is your God"? Answer him. Answer yourself. "He is in Rome. He is with me, precisely in this place, in the suffering, in the obstruction, in the difficulty, in the *meniah*. He is calling to me from the darkest, deepest, most difficult place in my life."

The Talmud is employing hyperbole but not exaggerating. Even there, even in that place in your life that is the lowest and most

Godless, filled with idols and filth, even there, God is in that place as well. What can a person do when he finds himself physically, mentally and emotionally in the "metropolis of Rome"? What recourse does he have when he finds himself overwhelmed by life's inevitable failures and frustrations? To be sure, he could try to avoid them or pretend that all is good and well, but that only prolongs the inevitable disappointment.

Like all good Talmudic answers, the more intrinsic solution to this question comes in the form of the question itself. "Where are you right now?" echoing the prophet Ezekiel, "Where is the place of your glory?" (*Ezekiel* 3:12) is an acknowledgement, that even in this very dark place, God is to be found. Indeed, that is where God must be found, for otherwise we will never find him. This point is critical to the understanding of *yishuv hada'at*. It is not that the answer is to be found in the form of another question. Rather, the question itself forms the basis of the answer. A person can be instantaneously revived by looking deeply into the distractions of life, further into his tumult and feelings of despondence and helplessness. The question isn't asked in a quizzical, uncertain fashion; the question is asked with the awareness that while I can't see it right now, I know you are right here with me.

The concealment of God is the driving force behind our despondence. And this concealment also serves as the primary source of the feelings of estrangement. Being stuck in whatever Rome presents itself comes from the feeling that at this moment, in this situation, the self is in fact bereft of meaning and God. If you are in spiritual or physical Rome, you might think you are bereft of God, bereft of the possibility of feeling God. Precisely then, the spiritual task that is incumbent on a person is to stop and just simply ask, "Where is the place of His glory?" even in that place, and proclaim, "God is here with me."

Of course there is no place empty of God. But the thickness of the mask of the "great metropolis of Rome" blocks and obscures any palpable sense of vitality and light; the lowest of all places, the epitome of concealment; a place where God is so hidden a person can feel that He is no longer even there at all. Precisely then the spiritual task that is incumbent on a person is to stop and just simply ask, "Where is the place of His glory?" – *even* in that place.

The moment a person asks this question, he brings himself back to the awareness that there are no places devoid of God, because there is no existence without God in the moment. The prayer of *Ain K'Elokainu*, begins, "None is like our God," and only then asks, "Who is like our God?" For when we ask the question, we already know the answer – as the Zohar says, "There is no place void of His presence," flows from the knowledge that "the fullness of the whole world is His glory" (Isaiah 6:3). Immediately, when a person begins to seek and ask, "Where is the place of His glory?" his question is answered, because the answer isn't in actually uncovering and finding. The answer is in the search and acknowledgement. Implicit in the search lies the immediate answer and salvation.

That heartfelt request is the acknowledgement that "I know that You are here right now, even in this place, no matter how dark and difficult the circumstances. I know that You are here even if I don't feel or see You." When I ask, I am fully acknowledging that You are here with me right now, for why else would I reach out to you? A person can therefore be at peace even in that very dark place, because now he is able to be in that place that once caused him to feel so distant, separate and alone, without being overcome by negativity. He is even able to be in that place and not forget who he is and what he believes in, and he can continue to feel the embrace of the One who never leaves us solitary and alone.

This is far from a passive choice. This questioning search requires strength and courage, along with the fortitude to know that often the answer will not readily present itself. And this is most definitely not suggesting that a person should meekly accept his lot, simply roll over and rely on God to handle it. It is a call to him, at that very moment, in that very place he is in, to just connect and ask, "Where is the place of His glory?"

Even while in Rome, regardless of how a person arrived there, any effort he makes to ask, "Where . . . ?" can instantly raze the walls he has constructed that separate him from his life source. Regardless of what happens after that moment passes – and he very likely will get swept up and separated again – a single gesture of seeking holiness is never lost. A person must bring himself back. He must ask himself again, "Where are you right now, and now, and now . . . ?" And he must understand that God is with him in each of those places.

Like the breath and the tides, there is a constant ebb and flow to life in which we all get lost from time to time. These feelings could be transitory or might last for years. Like our ancestors before us, we are tasked to travel a myriad of journeys to finally reach the Promised Land. It is not a question of how many oceans, rivers and swirling waters a person has to cross, or how many deserts and valleys we must pass through. It is a question of whether we can do all of this without ever losing sight of this belief: that no matter what, when and where, we can always find presence when we ask, "Where are you right now . . . ?"

When a person persists in his knowledge and belief that every single moment that he seeks to connect, becomes a moment of transcendence, then every place becomes a meeting place with the Divine and every *meniah*, a pathway to salvation. Each gesture and movement in which he searches for holiness and connection, regardless of circumstance, becomes infused with peace and purpose. When he asks, "Where is the place . . . ?" both he and God are simultaneously answering: "Wherever I am, right here, right now. With you."

A Reflection on Hindrances

"In my distress you relieved me." (Psalms 4:2)

That is, even in the distress itself, God provides us with relief. For if a person considers God's kindness, he will see that even while God causes him distress, within the distress itself God provides him with relief and increases his kindness for him. This is the explanation of "In my distress, You relieved me" – i.e., even in the midst of the distress itself, you provided me with relief from within it. Not only do we look to God to speedily save us from all distress and provide us with great good, but even within the distress itself we are provided with the expansiveness to see the relief itself.

(*Likutey Moharan* I, 195)

A song of David. The Lord is my shepherd; I shall not want. He causes me to lie down in green pastures; He leads me beside still waters. He restores my soul; He leads me in paths of righteousness for His name's sake. *Even when I walk in the valley of darkness, I will fear no evil, for You are with me;* Your rod and Your staff – they comfort me. You set a table before me in the presence of my adversaries; You anointed my head with oil; my cup overflows. May only goodness and kindness pursue me all the days of my life, and I will dwell in the house of the Lord for length of days. (Psalm 23)

Bi Adoni: The Lord is Within

BLISS. ECSTASY. RAPTURE. These are the words that the mind conjures up when a person tries to describe the ineffable experience of communing with the Divine Presence. It is what the spiritual seeker longs for. It is the elusive goal you and I chase day after day in our prayers, deeds and service. Most often, our labor leaves us feeling as if we have failed. We are left with the constant question: "All of this hard work, and for what? I feel the same as when I began." But then there are rare moments, often unplanned, when we experience the feeling that we had hoped for and more. The fantasy becomes real. And the warm embrace of the moment we had been seeking is right there for the taking. And we do everything we can to safeguard and deadbolt the experience to savor each precious second. Isaiah states:

> You shall seek the Lord where He may be found, call ye upon
> Him when He is near. (Isaiah 55:6)

This suggests that there is a moment and a place where God is found. And then inevitably, the moment passes. And what is a person left with? Can he feel anything but dejection and longing? Of course, our sentient mind comprehends that all things in life end and "this too shall pass." But does that cold, intellectual knowledge even remotely dull the pain? These are similar to the feelings which follow the elation of the High Holidays, the inescapable passage from ecstatic to mundane. While those feelings are seasonal and rare, for some it happens on an almost-weekly or even daily basis. In my house, I call it "the end of Shabbat blues." Every Saturday night there is that feeling that I hoped wouldn't recur but that inevitably shows up week after week without ever needing to be sent an Outlook reminder.

Often there is a direct and inverse correlation between the intensity of how ecstatic the holiday, the Shabbat, the prayer, or the moment was, and the precipitous, inevitable fall that follows. It is the all too familiar pattern of running and returning, the in breath and the out breath, the devastating waves that come crashing onto the peaceful shore. These daily ups and downs can cause a person to subconsciously wonder whether, perhaps, they would have been better off not experiencing the "high" to begin with. Is loving and losing really better than never having loved?

But we have seen this pattern before, a long time ago. And as always, we have our guide, the blueprint to our lives, to show us exactly what the appropriate response is to this all-too-painful challenge.

There is an extraordinary meeting between Abraham and God at the beginning of Genesis where this exact scenario plays out. Abraham had just dutifully followed God's command to circumcise himself and was sitting at the opening to his tent recuperating when God appeared to him. Just like that.

The commentators discuss the rationale for this impromptu Divine visit. Some explain that the sudden house call was most probably a result of God who, according to the mystics, also observes the Torah, fulfilling the precept of visiting the sick. But according to some of the commentaries, there was no rhyme or reason for this meeting. It was simply an expression of a genuine desire to be together. I don't need a reason to call my wife to tell her I love her or to call my mother to see how she is doing. God does not need a reason to visit His beloved Abraham. He does it just because.

All of a sudden, three weary travelers appeared in the distance. And even more surprising than their appearance was Abraham's response. Abraham's reaction was, in effect, to tell God, "Can you hold it for a second, please?" ("My lord, if I have now found favor in your eyes, I pray thee, pass not away from your servant" (Genesis 18:3)). If you have ever had time to think about the whole notion of call waiting, you have probably come to the conclusion that it is just flat out rude. Essentially, you are saying to someone, "There is something with the potential of being more important in my life than you right now, so be a dear and just hold on for a second while

I tend to something that might be more interesting, or more engaging, or more pressing. That would be just dandy." (And to add insult to injury, if you weren't sure of where you ranked in the list of this person's priorities, the music you are subjected to after someone puts you on hold often serves as a painful reminder that you are clearly not ranked among this person's top ten.)

This is all between two people. But this is Abraham and God, not Abraham and his mother-in-law. (I am not saying that putting your mother-in-law on hold is ok in that instance. I am just saying every circumstance should be judged independently.) This is the CEO of the entire world.

But without hesitation, in the middle of an intense embrace born of true affection – a hug, just because – Abraham says, "Do you mind? I have company right now. Three complete strangers."

How are we to make sense of this response? Isn't the essential purpose of our lives to be connected to God, to be connected to His presence at all times and in all things? Everything we do is meant to cultivate and deepen this relationship. It is to fully experience exactly what Abraham experienced. This was it: the zenith, the peak of all experiences. So how in the world could he ask God to wait?

The Rebbe of Kotzk famously once said, "God doesn't want more angels. He has enough angels." Angels are one dimensional and obedient – they have no choice. "What God wants is human beings." Being human is so much harder.

We are working towards the fruition of God's will that His presence be felt in this world, right here and now. In order to accomplish that, there will be times (actually, this proves to be the rule and not the exception) when, even in the midst of experiencing our own spiritual revelations, something will pull at our attention and say, "This is what you need to be doing right now." And suddenly the moment is transformed from a moment of "what I want to be doing," to "what must I be doing because the moment calls for it right now?" That is what He wants.

It is a delicate balance, this dance across the narrow bridge of life. From one second to the next, the response required of a person is rarely the one that he would have chosen from the start. I can vividly recall observing a teacher of mine who, while in the middle of what appeared to be ecstatic prayer, was able to respond with full presence to his child tugging at his coat, on the turn of a dime. He was wrapped up in God's embrace, but he knew that in that moment there was something more pressing. And that was what required his attention. To ignore what was calling to him, and persist in what he may have wanted to be doing, would have been to reject the call of that moment. Most important, like Abraham, he knew that God would approve. He had internalized God's value system.

After all that transpired during the enigmatic story of the binding of Isaac, the Torah tells that Abraham simply returned to his family. Everything he had gone through – the sleepless nights, the self-sacrifice, and the sublime, transcendental, spiritual level he had achieved – did not harm his ability to return to and be involved with the world right now. What happened a moment ago is gone. Right now I need to be a parent – granted, not the same one I was before – a changed parent, but one as equally invested and involved as ever in the rudimentary day-to-day details. Abraham did not become aloof or indifferent. These mundane experiences were not beneath him, because a genuine encounter with God creates closeness and deepens not only one's sense of responsibility but also one's response ability. For Abraham, this encounter with God deepened his ability to respond. In Judaism, all of the most amazing religious experiences in the world count for very little if a person doesn't remember how to connect to and deal with the day-to-day demands of life. If a person isn't able to retain this sense of being grounded, then in spite of all the amazing spiritual accomplishments he may have achieved, he has missed the point entirely. Desirable as it may seem, you can't spend your entire life at the summit. Like Abraham and Moses, you have to descend from the mountain. Without a doubt, Abraham, like all of us, felt the intense longing of wanting to prolong this experience forever. But he also understood that right now he needed to descend from his own personal experience and be with the people who needed him right now and be able to meet them at their level.

Even more deeply, Abraham's entreaty of God to "please hold," reveals a level of intimacy that only the most intimate of partners can request. Abraham was expressing, and instilling within all of us the ability to express, "I know that You came to visit me just because You love me, showing me the ultimate expression of concern and care. So I want to reciprocate this feeling. And we both know that I have to go and take care of my real-world concerns. Right now in front of me are three road-weary travelers, individuals who require my assistance and with whom I need to be involved. And I also know, because we are so close, that this is what You really want from me, and that I am imitating You to the best of my ability. You desperately want me to return from this crescendo to the minor notes of my life and be fully present and engaged in them. That's what You want from me right now, because that's what has been brought into my life at this moment. And I will leave this experience of revelation. I will leave this embrace. And I leave it willingly. But I ask You to help me, even though I am going back to the relatively smaller things of life, to feel Your presence in my life. And do not think for one moment that I leave unchanged."

If a person is able to stop in the present moment and realize that in the most seemingly insignificant and banal of times, God is still right there with him, then all he needs to do is be aware that in this moment he wants to maintain this closeness. True, it may not be the way it was before, it might not even be the ecstatic prayer or meditation that he had hoped for, but all of that was then and this is now – if he is able to bring his attention to what is really here in this moment, then he can transform any situation, no matter how trivial or inconsequential it is, into one of connectivity and warm embrace. Like Abraham, we take God with us into our lives.

A Reflection on Seeing the World

Initially Rabbi Shimon Bar Yochai and his son believed that the only practices that constituted *avodah* were Torah study, prayer, fasting and the like. Therefore, upon emerging from the cave in which they had spent years engaging in those activities and seeing people going about their workday lives, they became enraged, and said "They forsake activities dealing with eternal life and engage in the life of the moment." This attitude brought conflict and anger into their relation with the world, until a heavenly voice emerged and told them to return to their cave. They understood that they were being taught a new way of being in the world, a way of mercy. This path consists of is serving God through every aspect of every act, bringing awareness to the Godly presence found in every aspect of every act. This is manifest in the way that the masters of understanding are able to affect great unifications (*yichudim*) even in the midst of telling stories with friends or to remove sadness in the midst of engaging in business. Even upon seeing something unseemly in another person, or if someone or something were to distract us from our study and prayer, we should recognize that this too is from God, and for our benefit, in order to accomplish some Divine end through it. This is the more profound reading of "Know Him in all your ways" (Proverbs 3:6). Similarly as I have written to explain the verse "I place God before me always" (Psalms 16:8), means that even when I experience hindrances and opposition, nevertheless, "He is at my right hand, I will never falter." Therefore, "my heart rejoices" in arousing compassion and joy in the world and so "my body rests secure." (*Toldot Yaakov Yosef: Vayeitzei*)

Ad D'lo Yada:
Until He Doesn't Know

I F YOU KNEW that this would be the last time you were going to see your loved ones for an indefinite amount of time, what words would you want to leave them with, what message would you hope to convey? I imagine I would tell them how fiercely I love them and how nothing – no matter the distance or amount of time that passes – would ever change that.

This message was the exact one that God left with the Jewish people eons ago. Prophecy as our mode of communication with the Divine, was coming to an end. God's presence in the world would need to be sensed through a new medium. The final prophetic message was recorded and transcribed by the last prophet of the Jewish people, the prophet Malachi, whose prophecy presented God's parting conversation with His children, the Jewish people. Just as any devoted, loving parent would have done, God communicated all that He knew we would need to hear in order to hold us over in the long years of exile. These words were to be the parting gift, the words we would both need to hear and the words that God so badly would want us to have and keep in our consciousness until we would one day be able to embrace again. Words that would somehow be able not only to sustain but also uplift, in spite of thousands of years of separation and feelings of estrangement.

> I have loved you, saith the Lord. Yet ye say: "Wherein hast Thou loved us?" Was not Esau Jacob's brother? saith the Lord; yet I loved Jacob. (*Malachi* 1:2)

God's final direct written message to us was to simply say, "I love you." (And isn't that the only message that could really keep any relationship afloat over a few millennia?) But God knew that this message would also trigger a response. That response was our almost instinctive rejection of this sentiment. At this juncture in the relationship, with the impending separation of an indefinite time period looming, words like "I love you" seem to miss their mark. "If you loved me, you wouldn't leave me." Predicting and preempting our response, God therefore adds that He knows we will doubt His sincerity and question our own worthiness. "Wherein hast Thou loved us?" And can we be blamed? Look at our track record. "God, You more than anyone are fully aware of our sins, our failings, how unworthy we are of Your affection, of Your love. I am Esau's twin brother," we protest in our hearts and minds. And isn't that why You are departing from us? "How could You love us?" we ask. Experience and wisdom tell us that it cannot be true.

"You believe yourself to be Esau's brother" – God responds, "Not just a distant relative but a twin, the other half of the same coin. Indeed, you are part and parcel of Esau, the paradigm of the body, the material world, lust and sensuality, the aspects of your personal life and of the world around you that you wish you could disown. But can you see yourselves as I see you? Was not Esau Jacob's brother, yet I loved Jacob? Jacob, the symbol of the soul and the spiritual world. Can you see that in yourselves as well?"

We need to see in ourselves what God sees in us, and not accept the cognitive distortion that stops us from believing in God's infinite and immutable love for us. The "negativity bias" is a well-documented psychological phenomenon wherein people demonstrate greater recall of unpleasant memories than of positive memories. When a person looks at himself and focuses on how he is living, what he thinks, says and does, it is often hard for him to see how he is any different than Esau, and he often reaches the conclusion, "He is me. I am him." Consequently, it seems almost impossible for a person to have any other response to someone's admission of love than "How can You say that You love me? I wouldn't love me if I were You." This question may not be spoken aloud or even articulated in thought, but it is always lurking on the path of spiritual growth and development. "Am I truly worthy?" "Why should I believe in this love? How can I simply turn a blind eye to who I have become and what I have done?"

There are so many occasions for disbelief in our inherent worth.

When something goes wrong (and something inevitably goes wrong), when all I feel is removed from the presence of God, how am I supposed to believe in His love for me? "You want me to imagine that I am still very close to You and that what I do still matters and is meaningful, to believe that You love me, that my life makes a difference, that my actions make a difference? How is it that You can love me?"

Moments like these provoke this terrifying and depressing internal response, "the closeness and meaning that are our life's objective are meant for everyone but myself. This grace exists but remains unavailable to me." The Talmud speaks on a few occasions of the great scholar, Elisha Ben Abuyah, who became an apostate later on in his life and became known as Acher, "the other one." His ever-devoted student, Rabbi Meir, would often beg him to reconsider his decision, bringing his teacher proof after proof showing that it is never too late for repentance. And each time, his former master would end the discussion by responding, "I heard a heavenly voice that went forth and said: "'Return, my mischievous children' (*Jeremiah* 3:22). All of my children can return – all but Acher."

Even this towering rabbinic figure could do nothing to overcome this self-doubt: his guilt was so great in his mind that it could not be encompassed by God's love and forgiveness. Everyone could return, no matter how grievous his transgression, except for him. And so we defeat ourselves. For can we say that we don't feel the exact same way? When you do something really wrong, don't you hear the exact voice Acher heard? "The whole world can return to Me, the whole world makes a difference, the whole world can live in my presence, every Jew can affect all universes, except for you," says that voice inside oneself, in the exact same way that Acher heard that only he was ineligible to return, he alone could never come back after his misdeeds.

Have you ever tried comforting a distraught friend? I imagine you are able to extend empathetic encouragement with relative ease. But what happens when you are that distraught person? Would those same comforting words be as effective? The condemnation, "everyone but me" can be the most damning thought a person can have. Each of us knows too much about ourselves; only we know how guilty we are. This thought, which "crouches at the doorway," lurking in the mind, most poignant after a person has said or done something he thinks inexcusable, makes belief in this proclaimed love almost impossible. This clarity with which we think we see our-selves, ultimately becomes our blind spot. "How have You loved us?"

To make matters worse, this thought, this accusatory belief, doesn't come from anywhere or anyone other than ourselves. We do it to ourselves, and that's why it really hurts. "How could He love someone like me – forget about love, how about even *like* someone like me?" That question, that doubt, when a person begins to wonder what makes him worthy of being loved by God, brings all sources of impurity into his life. That's where the possibility of breaking the bond of the relationship with God begins.

"I love you," says God. But how are we to overcome our disbelief in this love? How can we cultivate acceptance of this immutable point? But the persistence continues. "Why should you love me? What have I done to deserve this? Have I ever done anything truly worthy of this love? I hear the words You are saying, but I just don't get it. It doesn't make sense." And the second this prophecy is no longer believed, what are we left with? Can we say that we believe? We need no reason to love our children, our siblings, and our par-ents, but we are unable to acknowledge the unconditional love of our Father in heaven. How can we overcome our natural reluctance to accept the Divine gift of love?

The way to cultivate this acceptance is to develop the capacity of "not knowing." The answer to this quandary is to be able to say "don't know." We are dealing with a love that surpasses comprehension. In order to offset this pervasive doubt and accusation, to purify this scurrilous impurity, a person must be able to live in a state of "don't know." Similar to the mindset of *temimut*, this does not mean that a person must live in a state of perpetual confusion, approaching life with a sense of doubt and befuddlement. Those attitudes will only serve to intensify the problem. A "not knowing" mindset means that a person is simply acknowledging that sometimes he does not need to understand something to believe in it. "Just as the Jews exclaimed, 'We will do and then we will understand' upon hearing of their im-minent receipt of the Torah at Sinai, I don't need to know everything before I accept it."

This attitude and state of being are reflected in the laws of the red heifer, which is understood to be the quintessential Torah statute that defies logic. King Solomon, the wisest of all men, was specif-ically referring to the red heifer when he wrote, "As wise as I am, possessing all of the wisdom of the universe, understanding the laws of the red heifer is still far away from me. I cannot grasp its meaning" (*Kohelet Rabbah* 7:23). While there is a plethora of laws in the Torah that defy any sort of rationale, the red heifer stands out as the most enigmatic. The essence of the law is that the ashes of the red heifer are used to purify those individuals who have contracted impurity through coming into contact with a dead body. But it is not this curious mechanism that puzzles the commentators. The most puzzling aspect of the red heifer is that the ashes of the red heifer can purify the spiritually contaminated, and contaminate the spiritually pure. The notion of the red heifer is that we live in a world filled with contradictory forces. How can it simultaneously purify the sullied while infecting the uncontaminated? How can evil come from good? How can good come from evil? "How can you love someone as corrupt as I am?" "I can know everything," says Solomon, "but this? This is far from me."

When a person looks at himself and asks himself, "Who am I?" and his response is that "it seems that I am no different from Esau, and yet You are telling me You love me even though I feel and look no different, that I can't understand. That is far from me."

In the realm of spirituality, distance and proximity are mere figures of speech. To say that something is close in the spiritual worlds does not mean that it is five minutes away as opposed to ten. When spatial terms are used in spirituality, they are speaking about resemblance. Two things that resemble one another are close in a spiritual sense, whereas things that differ are considered distant. Spiritually, the more that objects resemble one another, the "closer" they are.

So in that moment when a person looks at himself and his mind tells him that he is the same as Esau and that there is no reason for God to love him, he is obligated to say "I don't know." Any time a person tries to use human intellect to understand this, it will instantaneously be far from him. As soon as that intellect is suspended until he is in a state of not knowing, then and only then is it possible to feel that God indeed loves him.

Intellect is one of the hallmarks unique to humanity, but our intellect often traps us in the conundrums that our mind creates for us. In order to relate to some things that we are unable to understand, we paradoxically have to suspend our need to understand. There are things in life we don't understand, we can't understand, and yet we can still believe. "It doesn't always have to make sense to me. I'm never going to understand what this is completely about. But that does not for a second change this reality."

On Purim, there is a startling, anomalous, singular *mitzvah* to become inebriated "until one doesn't know the difference between 'blessed is Mordechai' and 'cursed is Haman.'" Some people take this quite literally, but a person needs to drink a lot to be unable to distinguish between the hero and the villain of the Purim story. The deeper meaning of this requirement is that Purim is a day to cultivate this attitude to last the entire year. Just as Shabbat is a day to cultivate the mentality of non-doing and acceptance, and inculcate it into the six days of the week, Purim is a day to nurture this attitude of "I don't know." Whether a person looks at himself and sees a blessed Mordechai or a cursed Haman, when he taps into the supra-rational place of not knowing, of not needing to know, he can become intoxicated with the realization that "we are Your heritage, and You are our lot" (High Holiday Prayer). God's name does not appear in the entire Book of Esther, which recounts the Purim miracle. Yet his unseen hand guides the salvation of the Jews. Unseen and unacknowledged, His love for His people pulses though the entire story. When a person enters into the world of the red heifer, a world that makes no sense, the lowest can be the highest. Another reality can be created instantaneously. At this moment he can feel that there is no difference between a Jew who looks like Haman and a Jew who looks like Mordechai. But God certainly knows. And we must know that God knows.

Of course, your mind is immediately starting to sling questions at you. Does it really make no difference if I am at my most Esau-like depths? I have a teacher who would tell us when this happens to "save your questions for the Seder night." Of course this attitude isn't an excuse not to be as good as we can be. But in order to want that and do that, in order to get out of the fixed mindset of unworthiness and the inquiry of "How have You loved us?" we have to start at a different place. First we must know that we are loved.

There is a hidden world beyond what we are able to see. And it is right here. And you can come to that place, says God. But as long as you are trying to "understand," it will be far away from you. When you recognize the capacity of "don't know", then you are right there, closer than you could have ever imagined.

Every time we engage in this type of self-doubt and self-critical behavior, we are once again engaging in the sin of eating from the Tree of Knowledge of Good and Evil. If you are a person who has to understand everything, your calculations may very often leave you feeling less than whole and way less than wholesome. As someone who has spent a lot of time with individuals suffering from anxiety, I know that they would all prefer to eat from the tree that makes it possible to understand everything. As much as we prize our ability to discern, even our superior intellect can become corrupt. But there is another tree, the Tree of Life, which says, unlike its counterpart, that you don't have to understand! If the meaning of a person's life is dependent on the Tree of Knowledge of Good and Evil, then life will only be considered worthy of living when he fully understands the person he is in a relationship with, the job he has, his parents, his children, his unique life circumstances, himself. He will never have the sweetness that is provided by the Tree of Life, when a person can love someone because "I don't always know and I can't always understand and it doesn't always show and it's not because of anything. Just because."

If you aren't prepared to cast away your need to understand (which does not mean that you must condemn yourself to being doubtful, confused, or dimwitted), your demand to understand everything just so, to make sense of everything, to insist on eating from the Tree of Knowledge, if you can't suspend that need to make sense, then you are stuck with the biggest question of all: "Why should God love me? It doesn't make any sense, when all I see when I look in the mirror is Esau."

You need to move beyond that. Regardless of the algorithm you use, if you simply can't let go of this need to know and that results in the belief that you are no different than Esau, then rejection and dejection are your inevitable companions in life. But if you can lift yourself up to a place of "I don't know" – and we all have the ability to do this – then you can once again start to love yourself, not because of what you do but simply because. It may seem so far away, but that is only because it is so far from your understanding.

> Rather, [this] thing is very close to you; it is in your mouth and in your heart, so that you can fulfill it.
>
> (Deuteronomy 30:14)

Yes, this belief is so far from your understanding, but "it is very close to you." Understanding is simply not the vehicle that can take you there from here. The ability to say "I don't know" at each moment of our lives answers all of the distortions and doubts. God loves us. God loves you. God believes in you. "Even though this doesn't all make sense to me, I accept that You love us. We are Your inheritance. We are together in this. We are Your congregation and You are our portion, we are your heritage and You are our lot. Even if I can't articulate why, I can't deny it either: in spite of not understanding, I know this is THE eternal message God chose to leave us with: 'I love you in an infinite way.'" When you surrender to the paradoxical feeling that God genuinely cares for and is deeply interested in your life, whether or not you understand His thought process you enter into the realm of not knowing, the realm of higher supernatural knowledge. And to survive and thrive, you have to believe in this message, and, most of all, feel that this love transcends all rational knowledge – "until he doesn't know. . . ."

A Reflection from the High Holiday Service

We are your people, and you are our God; we are Your children, and You are our father; we are Your servants, and You are our master; we are Your congregation, and You are our portion; we are Your heritage, and You are our lot; we are Your flock, and You are our shepherd; we are Your vineyard, and You are our keeper; we are Your handiwork, and You are our creator.

(Rosh Hashana High Holiday prayer)

"Thou art My servant, Israel, in whom I will be glorified."

(Isaiah 49:3)

Part III
Avodah
(With Each and Every Breath)

Modeh: Waking Up

J UDAISM TEACHES that "everything takes its shape from
the beginning" (*Pirkei DeRebbi Eliezer* 41). The beginning, that
initial spark of anything, contains within it all of its future out-
comes. "I will awaken the dawn," sings King David (Psalms 57:9). A
person is presented with a choice the instant he opens his eyes from
slumber: will he be the one to awaken the dawn or will the dawn
awaken him? With his decision, the seed of the day is planted, the
day is formed.

The purpose of *yishuv hada'at* is quite literally to wake up. The
choice to be with what is happening in the now occurs every time
we go from a state of mindlessness to one of mindfulness. One of
the most profound expressions of this occurs when a person exits
the hypnopompic state to enter one of wakefulness. Precisely in this
moment, in this critical movement from sleep to wakefulness, lies
the seed for the entire coming day.

Despite these grand ideas, the challenges with which a person
grapples with as he wakes up are usually standard fare. "Should I
open my eyes? Should I disregard the alarm clock and remain under
the covers? Can I get five more minutes of sleep?" Then, as he leaves
the bed, his ensuing stupor and careless fumbling do not seem like
an opportune time for any type of spiritual realization. But Judaism
stresses that precisely at this time there is an opportunity for something more.

The moment a person opens his eyes from sleep, his wakefulness
is accompanied by the implicit knowledge that he is alive. Being
alive demands a response. And that response, if a person is fully
present to this sense of aliveness, is one of gratitude.

It is precisely here that Judaism introduces the first prayer of the day, *Modeh Ani*: "I thank You, living and eternal King, for mercifully restoring my soul within me; Your faithfulness is great."

A Jew's first act of the day is to offer thanks. The first thing that a wakeful person does is say, "Thank you." This is what *yishuv hada'at* imbues within a person, a felt sense that we are eternal recipients of a gift and, that, implicitly, life is good. This feeling is wonderfully described by Abraham Joshua Heschel, who writes, "Our goal should be to live life in radical amazement. . . . Get up in the morning and look at the world in a way that takes nothing for granted. Everything is phenomenal; everything is incredible; never treat life casually. To be spiritual is to be amazed."

Modeh Ani. "I am grateful (or "grateful am I"). Not only am I expressing thanks, I myself, am an expression of thanks and gratitude. It is part and parcel of my essential identity." When Judah was born, his mother Leah said, "This time I will thank *Hashem*" (Genesis 29:35). The name "Judah" in Hebrew "Yehuda" means to thank. Our Sages explain that, in making use of this trait of gratitude, Leah passed it on to the Jewish people, who are therefore called "Jews" after "Judah." Judaism means essentially, giving thanks, being grateful. Our capacity for gratitude not only describes but defines us as well.

We have all been taught from an early age that when someone does something for us, it merits a thank you. I for one have an almost obsessive need for my children to say "thank you" when they receive anything, and granted, this might be my idiosyncrasy, but it is something I hope will become second nature to them, part of their persons.

In Hebrew, words contain layers of meaning. There is often an external usage and meaning to a word that also contemplates a deeper, inner understanding of the word. The Hebrew word for "thank you" is *todah*. More deeply, the word *todah* means "I acknowledge, I concede, I admit." Thus, in Jewish law, a litigant's acknowledgement of a debt, is referred to as *hoda'at baal din* – "the admission of the litigant." Essentially, he is saying, "I am *modeh* – I acknowledge, I concede, I admit – to your claim against me."

There is a profound relationship between these two meanings. Part of man's nature is to be fiercely self-reliant. In the depths of a person's soul there is an almost primal desire to be completely independent. One need to look no further than the closest two-year-old to hear the determined cry, "Do it *myself!*" This manifests itself not only in a child's developmental process but also in our relationship with God. Man's desire to be entirely self-sufficient precludes the possibility of relying on God in an absolute sense. We want to be our own agents. The expression "self-made man" is indicative of this mindset, a mindset that says, "I do not want to be beholden to anyone," a yearning not to depend on anyone but to rely on oneself alone. Man was created alone, and in the hidden recesses of our minds and souls we would like to remain that way.

Therefore, subsumed in the simple statement, *todah,* "thank you," is a profound admission that "I couldn't have done it without you. I am dependent on you." That gratitude is an expression of vulnerability, confession, and submission. Have you ever wondered why it is so hard for some people to say thank you? It is because in expressing their gratitude they are admitting that they need someone else and could not manage on their own.

Every time a person expresses gratitude he admits this: "I am not as independent as I thought I was. I really needed you." When a person gives thanks, he effects a seemingly magical transformation from an attitude of "it's all me" to one of "it's you too." And, then, inevitably, there is an "us."

There are psychological benefits to expressing gratitude, ranging from better physical health to improved mental alertness. But for the Jewish mindfulness practitioner, a person who desires to live a life of presence, these benefits are ancillary to the profound moment of connection with God that he achieves as he awakens.

A Story

When the holy rebbe from Apt (known as the Apter Rov) was asked how it was possible that it was already noon and he hadn't yet begun the morning prayer service, he replied, "I awoke hours before sunrise, but as I began to say the words *Modeh Ani*, "I thank You," I was struck by 'Who am *I*?' and 'Who is the *You* before Whom I am?' As I am still pondering these questions, I have not yet been able to go forward with my day."

(*Jewish Spiritual Practices* by Yitzhak Buxbaum)

A Reflection on Gratitude

After saying the words of *Modeh Ani*, stop for a moment and pause. Then say or think to yourself, "The power of the Creator is in His creation. The power of God is within each of us. If the flow of His life force ceased for a minute, we would disappear altogether, as if we had never existed. If that is so, how can we be lazy and lethargic in using this life-energy that He sends into us?"

(Rabbi Tzvi Elimelech M'Dinov, *Hanhagot Adam*)

Takum: Thoughts

H AVE YOU EVER SPENT any time just observing or cataloging your thoughts? Not lost in a hazy daydream or not trying to think of anything in particular, but actively paying attention to whatever you are thinking by just observing? If so, you might have been amazed, even shocked, to see how your mind is seemingly completely out of control.

Some people believe that *yishuv hada'at* means the ability to control one's thoughts or at least get rid of negative thought patterns. However, *yishuv hada'at* couldn't be further from this futile pursuit. *Yishuv hada'at* is not so much about control or elimination as it is about seeing clearly. When a person leads an unexamined life, his thoughts are what spur and drive him. They are both what he identifies with, and whom he identifies himself as being.

Therein lies the main obstacle to *yishuv hada'at*. For instance, a person might have thoughts (and their accompanying feelings) that what he is doing makes no difference, and that nobody really cares about him. He then becomes ensnared in the doubts and the misgivings that cascade through his mind and body, pulling him away from the things he most values, where he wants and needs to be focused. The results are often devastating.

The objective of *yishuv hada'at* is not to stop thinking (futile) or to banish all negative or "unholy" thoughts (equally ineffective). Attempts at this will almost always lead a person to falter just as he is beginning. The predicament of attempting to banish all unwanted thoughts has plagued man ever since Adam ate from the Tree of Knowledge of Good and Evil. Once again, we return to the very beginning.

After Adam and Chava ate from the Tree of Knowledge, God

called out to them with one word. It was in fact a question, to be more precise – the very first question asked in the Torah. Perhaps, just as the first time a letter or word appears in the Torah it expresses that letter or word's most profound meaning, the first question asked is the truest form of questioning, the precursor and embodiment of all questions.

This question is, *Ayeka*? "Where are you?" (Genesis 3:9). Now as you might imagine, God has a pretty good GPS system. And it wasn't as if there were a lot of people he needed to keep track of at the time. So this question clearly was not asking for Adam's coordinates. The question that was being asked is *the* question of our lives. This is the question that God asks each one of us at every moment and the question we need to be asking ourselves as well. "*Ayeka*?" Where are you? And with this question we can remove ourselves from doubt and from the ignominy of being mired in our thoughts.

Do you know where you are? God certainly knows, but do you? That one word, *Ayeka*, is all that a person needs to hear in order to snap out of the stupor and fog that results from eating from the Tree of Knowledge of Good and Evil, the tree of doubt and judgment.

Adam's response reveals the pernicious nature of his misdeed. "I heard your voice in the Garden, and I was afraid because I was naked, and I hid myself" (Genesis 3:10). Adam's fear was not that he wasn't wearing clothes, but the realization that he was exposed and uncovered. Suddenly he perceived himself as insignificant: exposed, naked of worth, bereft of value and substance. This feeling of exposure is more revealing and poignant than forgetting to put on your pants in the morning before you walk out of the house. This revelation to Adam was a radically new realization of how a person thinks and feels after having sinned. From that moment, he experienced complete identification with the ensuing pernicious thoughts and feelings, to the point that he feared that these beliefs would ultimately consume him. This fusion and identification with these self-negating thoughts constituted the most traumatic result of Adam's sin.

When a person has such thoughts, when he feels worthless, he instinctively, reflexively reacts by hiding. That hiding can take many forms: distraction, addiction, repression, sublimation, even delusion. This is how most people live, and then that becomes the story of their lives. When a person does not look at these thoughts and feelings properly, he can become enmeshed in a world created by the fruit of the Tree of Knowledge, which is the tree of doubt.

But whatever you may have done, felt or thought, God is always right there, saying "*Ayeka?*" *Ayeka* means, where are you at this very moment? Why are you so overwhelmed? Does this feeling of being completely lost and rejected really mean there is no way you can ever come back to your natural state?" *Ayeka* asks, "Can you see the causes that led to your thoughts and actions?" *Ayeka* asks, "Can you accept what you did, that you are not doomed to being permanently banished?"

God himself challenges the person who views his situation as hopeless, "Who told you that you were naked?" asks God (Genesis 3:11). God's question to all of us is, "does what you think and feel indicate objective truth?" Your actions may have been dire, but where does it say that you are worthless, that you have nothing, that your life is naked of significance and meaning? This negativity only comes from one source, says God: "Have you eaten of the tree, whereof I commanded you that you should not eat?" (Genesis 3:11). This response could have only come from a mind now tainted by having eaten from the tree of doubt.

And what transpired then continues to this very day. This is the "illusion" that the mind now presents to us. For a person to see things correctly, as they really are, he must expose himself to and be with ideas and feelings that can sometimes be extremely painful. But rather than doing that, a person often prefers, in some manner or form, to hide. Although he cannot hide from God, he can certainly hide from himself, from the realization that in order for him to be able to move in the valued directions of life, he will have to look starkly at what has led to his present situation and what is currently happening in his life, and start paying close attention to what is really happening. He is no longer able to contend with the learned helplessness of the pernicious belief that failure results from the "fact" that I am a failure and change is futile.

What distortions inevitably occur when a person thinks that he is a failure? The Torah describes the root of the distortions when man encounters failure in the story of Cain. "But to Cain and to his offering He did not turn, and it pained Cain exceedingly, and his countenance fell" (Genesis 4:5). Unlike the offering of his brother

Abel, Cain's offering did not find favor in the eyes of God. And so his "countenance fell" – dejected and rejected, Cain was the first person to experience depression. The source of his mental anguish was the belief that God did not care for his offering, and de facto, about him. All sense of abject failure is rooted in cognitively distorted thoughts, in the inability to see things clearly. The most common response that follows failure or disappointment is to conclude that what a person does, simply has no meaning. (The eminent cognitive theorist, Aaron Beck, describes a cognitive triad of negative thoughts that appear in depression: in which a person's cognitions are hopeless about himself, the world, and the future.)

God, seeing Cain's dejection, asks, "Why are you dejected? And why is thy countenance fallen?" (Genesis 4:6). God knows what is in the hearts and minds of men. The question to Cain was what is really causing you such distress? Are you able to look clearly at the thoughts and feelings that you now mistakenly believe to be inescapable and immutable?

God continues, "Is it not so that if you improve, it will be forgiven you? If you do not improve, however, at the entrance, sin is lying, and to you is its longing, but you can rule over it" (Genesis 4:7). God's question to Cain is: why are you so overwhelmed? You may have succumbed to a grave error in judgment. You need not let it result in any more destruction than has already been created. Cain however feels lost and rejected. Often a person gets fused with such thoughts and feelings, until his mind is seemingly filled with them, leaving no room for anything else, including the presence of God. This preoccupation is the most egregious error of not living with *yishuv hada'at*. Cain is so consumed by his feelings and thoughts of rejection and inadequacy that there is no room left for the council of God Himself.

And then the unthinkable can occur. A man can slay his own brother. Having done so, Cain was cursed, "A fugitive and a wanderer shall you be in the earth" (Genesis 4:12). Cain responded "My punishment is greater than I can bear . . . and it will come to pass, that whoever finds me will slay me" (Genesis 4:14). Make no mistake, Cain's concern wasn't just the imminent threat to his life. He now recognized that just as his urges, desires, thoughts and beliefs had annihilated him before, they could do so again. He was despondent, overwrought with the fear that this might occur again, afraid that

overwhelming thoughts and difficult emotions would take control
of and even "kill" him. Could that really be called "living"? In Cain's
belief that he was banished eternally from God's presence, that God
wanted nothing more to do with him, lies the root of all humanity's
depression and hopelessness about oneself, others, and the future. In
such a state, a person believes that he is so completely lost there is no
way that he can change and restore his life. Despite being alive, he is
a dead man walking.

> And the Lord said to him, "Therefore, whoever kills Cain,
> vengeance will be wrought upon him sevenfold," and the
> Lord placed a mark on Cain that no one who find him slay
> him.   (Genesis 4:15)

God's response to Cain was to place a sign upon him. The classical
commentators understand this to be some sort of physical mark,
while the Kabbalistic works say it refers to the Hebrew letter *vav*,
which is the letter that symbolizes the pillar of truth, and the Chasidic
masters say that it refers to the Sabbath, *Shabbat*. Regardless of what
the sign was, they all represent the same meaning. God told Cain,
"You might strongly believe that you are helpless and unable to mus-
ter any resilience, but I am still with you at every minute of your
life. Even when your thoughts and feelings are unsettled, 'wandering
and like fugitives' (Genesis 4:12), you can still find refuge by coming
back to what is, to being in tune with your body, to the experience
of truth, to remaining grounded and focused when you experience
Shabbat." (*Bereishit Rabbah*, 22:13)

We are no different than Cain. We would be fooling ourselves to
believe that we do not have and will never have such self-defeating
and dejecting thoughts. But what can a person do at the moment
that the "snake" appears in his life, when it seems that all that exists
are feelings of disgrace and unworthiness?

The first step is to recognize that there is *nothing* a person can
do to stop such thoughts from entering into his mind. But, as the
Greek philosopher Epictetus wrote, "It is not things themselves that
trouble us, but our thoughts about those things" (*Enchiridion*). The
hope of getting rid of transient "negative" thoughts and emotions is
more "magical thinking" than anything practical. However, behind
these thoughts and feelings, a person can discern his true being.

> There are many devices in a man's heart; but the counsel of
> the Lord, that shall stand (*takum*).   (Proverbs 19:21)

There are many devices in a man's heart, the thoughts upon thoughts that fill a person's heart, sometimes gently cascading and sometimes rushing like a fierce current. These thoughts never cease for even a second. What can a person do with this inescapable torrent of thoughts and emotions?

While many are the thoughts in a person's mind, the only true remedy is – as God advises in the verse – *takum*, to stand still. The enduring advice of God is to stand erect, unwavering and motionless. *Takum*. Let things happen just as they are.

God advises: Let your internal pictures, judgments and feelings arise and pass on without identifying with them. The way to respond to the perceived "ugly moments" of one's internal life is to look within oneself and contemplate. If a person becomes preoccupied and fused with the stirrings of his mind – be they in the form of thoughts, imagination, desire, lust or fear – he becomes mired in that thought. The more entrenched he is, the more he loses his *yishuv hada'at*.

If a person becomes preoccupied with those thoughts, even while he might engage in noble efforts to rid himself of them as "inappropriate," there can only be one inevitable consequence: his mind will grow more agitated. It is as though one has an itch, and the more he focuses on it, the more unbearable it becomes. By wishing it weren't there, he ensures its survival. If he despises and loathes it, he invites it to take up a more permanent residence. "Is it still there? How about now?" The more that a person's mind becomes involved and attaches itself to that thought, the more the thought is bolstered and cemented in his field of awareness.

Yet a person cannot just ignore it. If he could, he wouldn't feel stuck. He simply can't tell himself, "Don't have these thoughts," or "You shouldn't be having these thoughts." If you could just ignore them, the fields of psychology and meditation would quickly cease to exist.

People are often so adamant about eliminating these thoughts that they fail to consider that doing so is rarely, if ever, an option. (This phenomenon, known to practitioners of meditation for centuries, has been called the "theory of ironic processes" by Daniel Wegner of

Harvard University.) The more a person tries to erase these thoughts, the more they appear. And the more involved he gets, the more stuck he gets.

So what can be done? A Jewish meditative technique (see Appendix A) is for a person to shift his attention from identifying with the thought to viewing the thought. A person doesn't fuse with the thought, nor does he eliminate it. Instead, he observes it as it is. This is a subtle shift from not distinguishing between the thinker and his thoughts, to the person considering, "I am having a thought." This may sound easy enough, but for most people this task is all but impossible. A person is so adept at thinking, that he isn't even aware that he is doing it. And this ultimately is the most prominent result of Adam's having eaten from the Tree of Knowledge.

Stand still! Habituate yourself to step back and simply observe your thoughts. While a watched pot may never boil, a watched thought will simply dissipate.

When a person is able to do this, he no longer identifies with the thought or feeling. Instead, by taking a step back so that he may be able to observe it as it is, he has distanced himself from it – albeit not in an aggressive sense, or forcing it away. "I am not obsessing about it; I am thinking about it. I am not my thoughts. I am observing my thoughts." That distinction is the difference between life and death, hope and despair, slavery and freedom. By subjecting it to scrutiny and analysis you become its master, not its victim. You act on it. It does not act on you.

No matter how much I write about this, it needs to be experienced to be internalized. But when a person engages in this practice, he will quickly be able to see how, when he considers and examines a thought rather than thinking that he *is* the thought, it will dissipate on its own. (Take care not to keep checking whether the thought is still there or not, for that is a clear sign that you are identifying too much *with* the thought and not *about* the thought.) The more that a person fuses with a thought, the more inseparable he becomes from it, the more it dictates his every feeling and action, until he is trapped.

A person attains the freedom to ask himself *"Ayeka?"* when he undertakes the role of the questioning observer, investigating what he is thinking right now, when he is present so that he can stand still and ask, "What is true right now?" He is merely *observing* his thought rather than *being* the thought. His "I" is not the acted-upon person who is reacting, but the observer. His ego is subtracted. And when that happens, the grasp of his thoughts on him is also weakened. Often, the thought disappears entirely. But even if the thought remains, its paralyzing grip is inestimably weakened. This idea is critical in the field of psychopathology. But for our purposes it addresses what is often the primary impediment to a person's spiritual growth.

When you view your thoughts and feelings as an outside observer, there is no longer any self-involvement that demands their removal. Those feelings or thoughts don't lose their true nature. They are, in fact, very real. Rather, all of the additional components superimposed upon them are recognized and made fully conscious.

There is a widespread popular slogan that stresses that a person should endeavor to "be here now," expressing the need to live in the present moment. And while few would disagree with the value of doing so, the problem is exactly how to fully inhabit this present moment. Our minds dwell mostly in the past and the unknowable future. However, the way to contend with this – and, even more importantly, to bring an attitude of balance and awareness into one's life – is to cultivate this mindset of *takum*, of just standing still and observing. Then a person no longer has to hide from the tension of attachment or dislike that arises in the mind spending too much time avoiding the feelings of worthlessness and deficiency. Rather, he is able to be with things as they are. This attitude is not limited to the times that a person is sitting in quiet contemplation. This mindset of *yishuv hada'at* needs to permeate our actions and interactions, so that it serves as the backdrop for all of life's experiences.

This is the foundation for any spiritual endeavor. A person can only begin working on himself once there has been an infusion of that which is true and holy, his essential immutable goodness and the fully internalized realization that the place where he stands is holy ground. First you have to let God in. This does not have to mean that life and its challenges will always be positive or feel good. But once he is clear on who he is in reality, then and only then can he go back and honestly face the parts in himself that are unhealthy.

There is a certain point in the practice when the momentum of mindfulness is so strong that it starts working by itself, and we begin to do things with an ease, simplicity and naturalness which is born out of this effortless awareness. Bare attention is very much learning how to listen to our minds. At first, all we can hear is a single "self" or "I." Slowly, this self is revealed as a mass of changing elements, thoughts, feelings, emotions and images, all illuminated simply by listening, by paying attention, revealing the essential I, the Divinity that resides within.

A Story

One day a few of the students of the holy Baal Shem Tov came to him with a question. "We travel great distances to come here to learn with you, Master. Nothing could ever stop us from doing that. But we have been told that there is a man in our town who claims to be a *tzaddik*, a righteous, enlightened individual. If he is truly a *tzaddik*, we would greatly benefit from learning from him. How can we tell if he is who he says he is?"

The Baal Shem Tov looked at his earnest Hasidim. "You must test him by asking him a question." He paused. "Have you ever had difficulty with stray thoughts during prayer?"

"Yes!" The Hasidim answered eagerly. "We try to think only of our holy intentions as we pray, but other thoughts are always entering into our minds. We have worked on the many methods you have taught us so as not to be distracted by them."

"Good," said the Baal Shem Tov. "Ask him the way to stop such thoughts from entering your minds." The Baal Shem Tov smiled. "If he has an answer, he is a fraud."

(Jewish Spiritual Practices by Yitzhak Buxbaum)

(See Appendix A: Hashkatah)

B'ruchim HaBa'im:
Welcoming Our Selves

H AVE YOU EVER HEARD of an angel needing to go to therapy? No one ever hears about an angel suffering from a nervous breakdown or a panic attack. Could it be that angels are immune to emotions?

> "Then they all accept upon themselves the yoke of the sovereignty of heaven one from the other and lovingly grant permission to one another to sanctify the One Who formed them, with calmness of spirit, with articulation that is clear and with sweet melody. All of them as one proclaim sanctification with trepidation and say with fear, "Holy! Holy! Holy!" (Morning Prayer Service)

On the contrary, it appears that angels are able to experience the full range of emotions – fear, trepidation, love – seemingly, whatever the feeling might be, all the while remaining angels. How can one experience a full range of emotions, yet remain saintly, beyond temptations of frailty? The answer is that angels don't experience – or, more precisely – angels are not overwhelmed by panic. The sages teach that an angel can only perform one mission at a time. The actual translation of the Hebrew word for angel is messenger; an angel carries one, and only one, message at a time. Angels are therefore designed to be the antithesis of multi-tasking. Additionally, every angel knows what is expected and required of him at every moment, so all that exists for an angel to do in the world is the task at hand. His entire being is filled with the presence and purpose of the present moment. Everything an angel does is imbued with the awareness of the spiritual emanations of each moment. Living in the constantly felt presence of God, the angel has an existence that is continuously bursting with purpose and meaning. He is filled with that moment and with the task designated and appropriate for that moment. Consequently, he can feel the full range of emotions – fear, love, wrath, and trepidation, without being diverted – because he fully occupies the place he is in. An angel is always living with the quintessential expression of *yishuv hada'at*.

A person's emotions and their interchange with his sense of self are typically involved in a tricky feedback loop. There are even traditional sources that, if not studied properly, seem to decry certain emotions as bad, evil and sinful. So if you happen to experience any of these emotions – which, I assure you, will inevitably happen – and your relationship to these feelings is one of non-acceptance and rejection, then you will do everything in your power to get rid of them. Related to this is the even more potentially damaging belief that these feelings imply a judgment about you. If you have been conditioned to believe that only an unrefined or unspiritual type of person feels anger, jealousy, and lust, the experience of these emotions will brand you as a deficient being. And thus you have opened up a Pandora's box of self-recrimination, self-doubt and guilt. Once these feelings have arisen, a person is sapped of any resolve to grow. This is inevitably followed by a vicious cycle of identifying with or fruitlessly attempting to suppress these feelings, feeling guilty and regretful, struggling to overcome the guilt, and, once the feeling arises again, experiencing the process all over, again and again.

Current research in psychology demonstrates that every emotion serves an adaptive function. It exists to teach a person both about our inner life and our relationship to our surroundings. In the mystical works of Judaism, the expression that "evil does not descend from the heavens" describes our relationship to emotions. Put simply, there is no such thing as a "bad" emotion. However, when a person relates to an emotion in an unhealthy way – be it through neglect or becoming overly preoccupied with it – this emotion is said to have fallen.

For example, fear is an emotion that is adaptive, helpful and constructive. If a person doesn't feel fear when he sees a bear approaching, there is a good likelihood that he will not have a chance to tell anyone how he narrowly escaped the encounter. But what if you start to feel afraid every time you leave the house, thinking you are going to run into the bear again, to the point that you can no longer leave the house?

In the course of one's spiritual development, emotions can be used constructively in the service of cultivating one's development and growth. But if these emotions are not properly attenuated and refined, they can become what the mystical works refer to as "fallen." Each emotion has its source and root in a Divine realm such as loving-kindness or strength. It was conceived in innocence and purity. But when that emotion falls away from its source, the consequences can be negative, even destructive. A person who lives in a constant state of anxiety is in a place of "fallen fear." The source of worry is *gevurah*, which is also the source of one's ability to be God-fearing. When properly channeled, this trait imbues a person with a sense of awe and wonder. But when fear and anxiety dominate, then the "fear" is said to be fallen.

Chesed is the source of a person's ability to love and direct his love towards the proper objects. But if you love the wrong people, places, and things, then that love has fallen. When the love overwhelms you to the point that it spills over into areas where it creates suffering, that love is said to have fallen. Emotions are essentially good; unchecked emotions are dangerous.

How does one elevate an emotion? For instance, how do we elevate ourselves from the misery of unhealthy anxiety, worry, and fearfulness? Note that Judaism never promotes uprooting or excising these "negative" emotions. This is a crucial distinction. The point is never to try to get rid of what is already there, but rather to elevate. Judaism does not define any particular emotion as good or bad, but rather views it as a force that needs to be channeled. If a person cuts off a part of himself, he becomes an invalid. When he elevates that part of himself, he brings it (and ultimately himself) to completion.

In order for a person to elevate his emotions, he must become an expert observer, similar to an appraiser looking at a precious item, able to observe without becoming attached. Our emotions are lifted with the quality of "evaluation." Normally, "evaluating" and "judging" evoke images that connote taking a harsh and critical stance. But the judgment we are recommending is not an emotional process. It is an observation guided by an attitude of curiosity and openness. Exact judgment requires unflinching honesty, but also objective detachment. A judge who has a bias or personal preference in a case must automatically recuse himself. So too, when we are judging our emotions, the evaluation must be done without judgments. Our sages teach that when one is acting as a judge, he should take caution not to act as a lawyer would but rather he should remain impartial. This teaching also applies to our own thoughts as well. One should not act as his own litigator when he is examining himself, but should, instead, be as objective as a judge. (*Avot* 1:8)

When a person begins this process, when he starts to ask what is true right now, he will see how his emotions can be experienced, seen, and felt as they truly are. The more familiar and honest we are in our relationship to these fallen emotions, the more easily we can feel, as do the angels, grief uncomplicated by despair, joy that is unadulterated, or any emotion having it mixed up with guilt, anger, remorse, embarrassment, judgment or other sentiments.

Emotions are there to guide us – sometimes to point us in the right direction, and at other times to highlight which path we should not be taking. *The problem is never with what we are feeling; the only problem is with how we relate to that feeling.* If a person accurately judges himself, if a person is completely present to what he is feeling and is able to sensitize himself to what's going on internally, then regardless of what is transpiring in his internal world, he will be able to remain on the course he has set for himself.

No one will get through life without experiencing the pain and pleasure of intense emotions. But if a person is able to raise his emotion to a place where he can see what is truly happening, to a place of *yishuv hada'at*, to the ability to know what is true at this moment, to the felt experience of whatever he is undergoing, then no matter what happens, his emotions while always remaining a part of him, will never engulf and consume him.

As with all of these ideas, this is an experiential teaching, and as such needs to be experienced and practiced to be fully understood. A person who is concerned with his obligation in the world right now, with what is happening in the present moment, is able to evaluate in a calculated and measured way rather than in a critical or condescending manner. That person is able to liberate the emotions that have fallen away from their connection to the present. Once he is freed of distorted fear and love which takes the form of anxiety and addiction, anxiety and terror, a person can be at peace, knowing just what is.

When a person gets caught in the multitude of calculations rather than just being with what is, he can forget his essential self. Being upright is our natural state. While it is true that we cannot be angels, we can emulate their angelic ways: to have the *yishuv hada'at* with which to be fully aware of what we are experiencing and really see what is true right now.

> Behold, this only have I found, that God made man upright;
> but they have sought out many calculations.
>
> (*Ecclesiastes* 7:29)

A Story

One time, after the Romans had ravaged Jerusalem and destroyed the holy Temple, Rabban Gamliel, Rabbi Elazar ben Azaria, Rabbi Yehoshua and Rabbi Akiva went up to Jerusalem. When they reached Mt. Scopus, they tore their garments. When they reached the Temple Mount, they saw a fox emerging from the place where the Holy of Holies had stood in the Temple. The others started weeping, but Rabbi Akiva laughed.

They said: "Why are you laughing?"

He replied, "Why are you weeping?"

They said to him: "This place [is so holy] that 'the stranger that approaches it shall die' (Numbers 1:51). Now that foxes traverse it, shouldn't we weep?"

He told them: "For the same reason you are crying, I laugh. A verse states, 'and I will take unto Me faithful witnesses to record, Uriah the priest, and Zechariah the son of Jeberechiah.'" (Isaiah 8:2).

Uriah lived in the time of the First Temple, and Zechariah in the time of the Second Temple. So what is the connection between Uriah and Zechariah? But, by referring to them both together, the prophet makes his prophecy regarding Zechariah dependent upon that regarding Uriah. A verse states regarding Uriah, 'Therefore, because of you, Zion shall be plowed as a field [Jerusalem shall become heaps, and the Temple Mount like the high places of a forest.]'

(*Michah* 3:12); and a verse states in Zechariah, 'Old men and women shall yet sit in the streets of Jerusalem' (*Zechariah* 8:4).

"As long as the prophecy regarding Uriah had not been fulfilled, I feared that the prophecy regarding Zechariah might not be fulfilled. But now that the prophecy regarding Uriah has been fulfilled, it is certain that the prophecy regarding Zechariah too will be fulfilled."

Hearing these words, they replied to him: "Akiva, you have consoled us! Akiva, you have consoled us!" (*Makkot* 24a–24b)

The ability to simultaneously experience the joy of the ultimate redemption and the pain of the destruction is the secret to Rabbi Akiva's laughter. To be sure, Rabbi Akiva was not a callous individual, insensitive to the heartbreak of the Temple's destruction. He experienced the tragedy as intensely as did his colleagues. But within that tragedy, as within all experiences, there was something more to be discerned. Rabbi Akiva was open to the full gamut of emotional possibilities finding a balance in life, tempering destruction with the possibility of redemption. He did not ignore or disavow the feelings of loss and pain. They are real. And yet, "for that very reason, I am laughing" – because he recognized that *within* the pain and suffering, *together* with the pain and suffering, and *despite* the pain and suffering, there was also meaning. And then there could be true comfort.

A Reflection on Emotions

When a person's emotions are aroused, or if something external has generated an emotional reaction, he should not heed his first instinct to compulsively seek out some physical satisfaction. (For example, if you feel slightly anxious, do not think you are hungry and run to find something to eat.) Instead, observe and attend to the feeling and see what it is. If the feeling is one of lowliness and brokenness (depression), then look carefully within and investigate where this feeling is from: "Perhaps I committed some sin recently, or did something low, or said or thought something improper. I am unable to even remember exactly what it was that produced this sadness because everything I do in my life is done in a hurried fashion, and all the years of my life are passing quickly and in confusion. And due to this transgression, whatever it may be, my soul feels smitten and has become sick. And the soul is crying out from the deep pain it is experiencing, causing this feeling of deep pain and sadness."

Therefore, when such a thing happens, after a little investigation, you will find something you did or thought. "I did this improper deed, or I said or thought something improper." There is a clear sign that will tell you when you do find the true cause of your feeling, because the moment that you detect and identify the true cause of your feeling, it will lift from your heart. By finding it, acknowledging it, by honestly looking at it – that will bring some degree of relief. But do not be satisfied with this discovery alone. You also have to accept the obligation not to make this error again. Merely accepting not to do this anymore, will not suffice. One must accept additional stratagems to overcome the problem as well.

Whether you find the source of your feeling or not – regardless of the type of emotion you experience – or whether it is a feeling that is intrinsic or aroused from something external – be compassionate to yourself, do not just ignore this feeling and move on. Your soul has revealed itself somewhat in this feeling. Be quick to strengthen this glimpse into the soul. Take hold of it and do not let it go. Expand the feeling and say some psalms that fit the mood so that this feeling will expand in breadth and depth, so that it will be sharper, and will remain and not disappear in a flash.

(*Hachsharat Ha'avreichim*, Chapter 9)

Mitzvot: Remembering to Remember

THERE IS A MODICUM OF TRUTH to the old saying, "Two Jews, three opinions." The Jewish people, the people of the book, are known for having strong beliefs and opinions, and are rarely shy about letting their views be known. In the myriad of disputes in the Talmud, there remains one agreed upon precept – which, considering the Talmud's penchant for arguments, is an amazing phenomenon in and of itself.

There is complete agreement that there are 613 *mitzvot* (ethical precepts or prescribed ritual actions). There is not even a single dissenting opinion among the commentaries that suggests otherwise. There is also complete agreement that these 613 *mitzvot* are divided into 248 positive *mitzvot* (one for each bone and organ of the body) and 365 negative *mitzvot* (one for each day of the solar year). (Before we get carried away with all of the harmony, there is not 100% agreement on the precise list of the 613, as there are slight discrepancies in the way various commentators list related or overlapping *mitzvot*; we are, after all, still talking about Jews.) The number 613 is the magical number for the commandments. It is undisputed and immutable – and so . . . large. The number is so sizeable that it almost reflexively kicks off feelings of resistance. "How can I be expected to keep track of, let alone observe, all of them?" It is in our human nature to be proud, free and unfettered. Our earliest recollections are of when we asserted our own independence in order not to be subservient to the demands of others. Freedom and liberty are among our most desired traits. Philosophies have been built on free will as the defining characteristic of the human being. And here comes the Torah with – how many commandments again?

The Talmud teaches, "Rabbi Simlai, when preaching, said: 613

precepts were communicated to Moses: 365 negative precepts, corresponding to the number of solar days [in the year], and 248 positive precepts, corresponding to the number of the parts of the body. King David came along and condensed the commandments to eleven. The prophet Micah further condensed them to three. The prophet Isaiah further condensed them to two. Finally, the prophet Habakkuk condensed them to one – i.e., 'A righteous person will live by his faith'" (*Makot* 24a). The multitude of laws, restrictions, prohibitions, and adjurations can all be distilled into one pristine principle: faith. So which is it – 613 or 1?

In the *Zohar*, the 613 *mitzvot* are referred to as 613 elements of advice, all guiding us to one destination. Somehow, each one of the 613 provides a light of guidance drawing us closer to God. The end game is not fear or even love of God (each of which is its own unique commandment) but rather something greater. *Every mitzvah is, in its own way, a means of forging a connection to our consciousness of God's presence in our lives so that we never forget, but instead always remember to remain wholly attached to God.* With this understanding, it is possible to distill the 613 pieces of advice into one general behest, one overarching theme. Faith is the ultimate connection a person can have with the Holy One; the essence of faith is always feeling and being connected with God. The person who lives with faith in God is effectively connected with Him at all times. The *mitzvot* are a reminder of God's immanence: indispensable, essential, and necessary methods for constantly reminding us of God's presence in our lives.

Man was created in God's image. Considering the fact that God is an omniscient, transcendent being whose likeness cannot be compared with anything physical, makes Divinity different from any entity you and I have ever encountered. And yet God Himself says that we are created in His image. Clearly, our resemblance to God must not be evident in how we look, but rather in what we do. *Imitatio dei*, trying to behave (so to speak) as God would behave, distinguishes humans from animals and believing humans from those whose untethered lives have no fulcrum.

The most profound expression of that Divine similarity is that a human being, much like God, has the power to create. Even while an animal can procreate, construct dams and build hives, those endeavors are nothing more than an outcome of an animal's instinctive nature. Man, on the other hand, can choose to create, and with that a human being has the ability to change the world, precisely as God desires. Unlike God, human beings cannot create something from nothing, *ex nihilo*, but we are at our most Godly when we are creating and forming.

There is, however, a danger in this power, for – as the expression goes – power tends to corrupt. Man can use this creative ability to change the world for good or conversely use it for destructive purposes. The midrash tells that immediately after God created Adam, He raised him up and "showed him each of the trees in the Garden of Eden and told him: 'See My works, how good and excellent they are! Now all that I created is for your sake. Think upon this. Do not corrupt or destroy My world, for if you destroy it, there will be no one to restore it after you'" (*Kohelet Rabbah* 7:19). The midrash's message is clearly implied: inherent in the awesome power to create is the converse power to destroy and corrupt.

The greatest danger that exists when wielding this Divine quality is the unfortunate tendency to become so infatuated, so intoxicated with the power of creation that one ultimately forgets the true Creator. One of my teachers once remarked, somewhat in jest, that there is no such thing as an atheist. In actuality, everyone in the world believes in a god. Some however, make the fatal mistake of believing that the Divinity that resides within us is not distinguished from his or her own self. With our creative abilities, a person can begin to think that he is, indeed, God.

Thus, the ability to create engenders a tremendous danger and risk that man might ultimately see himself as the Creator. The possibility exists that he will become so impressed by his own power, his own God-granted volition, that he will simply forget the true Creator. He will reach a point where he begins to believe that "my power and the might of my hand have gained me this" (Deuteronomy 8:17) – wealth, job promotion, success – you name it. Everything that you see now is a direct result of "my" strength, power and ingenuity, which alone are responsible for the creation of this reality. We look in the mirror of our soul and we see only ourselves. We selfishly give up the gift and privilege of seeing God in us, or us in God.

When is a person most likely to be overly impressed with his power to create? When he sees something change before his eyes. Until a few hundred years ago, this would occur most frequently in the fields, orchards and pastures. When a person is fertilizing the soil or trimming the weeds, furrowing and plowing, there is little hubris to be found. But when he starts harvesting the produce, suddenly a change has taken place: there is something where there was nothing. When he sees he has the power to transform, *ex nihilo*, like God, he is susceptible to becoming enthralled with himself and his capabilities. That extraordinary change that is taking place, precisely where he invested his ingenuity and energy, creates the potential for him to see himself as solely responsible for this new outcome. A person doesn't need to be a farmer to experience this phenomena. If, after a sales pitch or after performing an operation or prescribing medication, one sees change, it is hard to remain humble. The feeling of control a person experiences when they are involved in creating change, in controlling events, is often accompanied by the danger of forgetfulness. One can easily imagine how doctors, psychologists, salesmen, artists and entrepreneurs can easily become susceptible to this trap.

Of course, one should feel good about one's accomplishments. One should take pride in the hard work and the time invested in one's career and life's objectives. It's just that at the moment that something changes, if one isn't mindful, one is very likely to feel a sense of separation from the Master of the world, and the de facto feeling that ensues is an overinflated sense of your own power. You are not God; you are God's partner.

All of Your *mitzvot* are faithful.   (Psalms 119:86)

This is how all of the *mitzvot* can be concentrated into one basic *mitzvah* that is all-encompassing: the *mitzvah* of faith in God. From God's perspective, the *mitzvot* are all one. Simply put, if you do a *mitzvah*, any *mitzvah*, you acknowledge God in your life. Just as He is one, His will is one. The *mitzvot* reflect the unity of God's will, as well as the means of attachment to this will. While they may seem disparate and separate to our intellects, at their root and core they are all manifestations of faith. The *mitzvot* of not wearing linen and wool together and honoring one's parent, so different from each other, unify us with God, because they are the commandments of a living, present God.

Thus, we see how God is advising us with 613 pieces of instruction and guidance, each one forming a unique way to remember Him. This approach is not based on our rational ability that attempts to discern the purpose of each *mitzvah* from a logical perspective (though that too brings us closer to God). *This is about cultivating an approach to the mitzvot from the perspective and belief of how each individual mitzvah attaches a person to the Divine right now, even if he doesn't understand and quite possibly even if he doesn't feel like performing it.* The *mitzvot* are about developing a mindset to constantly be aware of how this action applies to my life *right now*. Every opportunity to perform a *mitzvah* found in the Torah is really telling us another avenue to connect to God in every aspect of our lives. Even when we might not practically be able to fulfill a certain commandment, the concept still reveals something to us on a deep and personal level of how to remain attached to God.

> Lest you go astray and serve other gods. (Deuteronomy 13:13)

The *mitzvot* are built-in sacred pauses to our days and years; they use objects and are performed in spaces – and in these ways they remind us to once again stay connected to the source. The farmer working in the field is not required to tithe until the moment the produce is organized into bushels and stacks. Before this work is done, the farmer is not saturated with the deep sense of profound accomplishment. Now that the job is effectively done, the farmer is able to sit down, wipe his brow, and think about himself. "Blessed are You, the One Who has brought the dead back to life." "Look what I have done: I've taken a barren piece of land and I brought vitality to it." The moment of change from empty furrows to stalks of wheat attached to the ground to wheat ready to be sold or used, contains the potential for severing the connection between man and God. It is precisely then that there is a commandment to tithe. When the natural inclination would be to protest and say, "I have to give it away? I made it. It's mine." Right in that moment there is a command to remember, to pause. "Before anything, stop and give it to the priest, the Levite and the needy."

At that moment of change, when a person feels that transformation taking place, precisely then is he most apt to forget, most susceptible to lose his faith. God says, "Remember." Each *mitzvah* is a reminder. "Don't forget." Forgetfulness is that point where a man

is most tempted to say, "of my own power that brought this about."
Here is where God gives us his "advice" – precisely at the point when
a person can be drawn away. That advice, that *mitzvah*, is meant to
bring a person back. Do not forget! Do not get pulled away! Put on
tefillin. Say the grace after meals. Each disparate *mitzvah* forms the
bond of remembrance.

One can apply this principle to every one of the 613 *mitzvot*.
While it is beyond the scope of this book to discuss how each of
the *mitzvot* serves to deepen this consciousness, a few examples will
demonstrate this idea clearly. The commandment to wear *tefillin* on
our arm and head, opposite the heart and mind, are to be a constant
reminder of awareness, in spite of the illusory control we feel that
we are the sole decision makers and arbiters of our own destiny.
God therefore commands us to don *tefillin* on our head and arm
to remember that your thoughts and deeds should be done with
intention and awareness of His presence. The blessing recited when
putting on the *tefillin*, reflects this mindset. The blessing uses the
unique phrasing of "*lihaniach tefillin*" the resting of the *tefillin*, to
not just mean the placement and binding of the *tefillin* but that they
should rest in a person's awareness, so that he will be conscious that
this is a moment to remember. In spite of the natural inclination
to believe that I create by my arm, by my strength and brute force,
or that through my innovation, creativity and ingenuity I develop,
through my *tefillin* I am reminded that all of these creative acts are
through You.

> And you will see it, and remember all the *mitzvot* of *Hashem*,
> and perform them.   (Numbers 15:39)

The reminder the Torah refers to is the strand of *techelet*, sky-blue
dyed wool that is attached to the corners of any four-cornered garment. This strand serves as a reminder, a visual meditative device,
"for *techelet* is similar to the sea, and the sea is similar to the heavens,
and the heavens compare to the Throne of Glory" (*Menachot* 43b).
"This similarity is in name (the word *techelet* is similar to *tachlit*,
'purpose') and in color. And from a distance, everything appears
that color. Therefore, it is referred to as *techelet*" (Ramban, Numbers
15:38). The *tachlit* – purpose – of the *mitzvot* is to infuse emotion into
the heart and mind so that a person will always remember – not in

a passive sense but with an active vigilance, paying attention to what is happening right now. A person can look at a strand of sky blue and must remember that this strand in my hand binds my awareness together with the ocean, the sky, the throne, God's presence. This contemplation exercise isn't limited to the specific *mitzvah* of *techelet*. This mindset can be applied to all of the *mitzvot*. Each one in its unique way contains advice on how to look at everything in the world and see that there is nothing separate, there is nothing that cannot be lifted up to its purpose. By a little blue strand, be reminded, be conscious that there is an ocean, and there is a sky, and there is a world, and there is a Master of the universe. That little piece of strand you wrap around your finger not to forget, reminds you always to remain mindful of what we are doing here.

A person can get so lost in the little pieces, or his own accomplishments, that he forgets about the ocean, forgets about the sky and forgets there is a Creator. Without this sensitization, we become detached from God's world and imagine that we are alone. *Mitzvot* demand that a person make the time to contemplate this. Without constant and repetitive *practice* it, it just becomes rote action and eventually meaningless.

Every *mitzvah* is meant to wrap our awareness up once more in the presence of the Divine. Even when there is no chance of forgetting, a person must remain vigilant. This is the *mitzvah* of the first fruits (*bikurim*), which are consecrated even while they still remain on the tree, when a person ostensibly does not need a reminder. The *mitzvah* of *bikurim* is not there to prevent a person from forgetting. It reminds him to pay attention even as he is moving on to the next stage, because moving to the next stage is also a time when preoccupation and forgetfulness can set in. Stop here now, in this stage of the growth process, so that when the separation inevitably occurs, in the midst of that upheaval and confusion of the world of work, life, and family, you won't forget. We need constant reminders to ward off the persistent urge to forget.

In telling us what we need to do to cultivate our relationship with God, each *mitzvah* is another way to deepen our relationship with Him. The closer you are to someone, the more nuanced the relationship becomes. How can strands of wool serve as a reminder of all the *mitzvot* and all that they entail? It is because in a deep, real relationship there are no longer any aspects that can be considered "small things." Sensitivities, care, concern – the interaction between two people who love one another deeply may look odd to the outsider, but to those individuals, every gesture and look is saturated with meaning. It is the *mezuzah* by the doorpost, as you go out into the world of confusion. Touch the name of God and remember before you go outside. Remember God when you enter and when you leave. It could be just a perfunctory gesture but with a proper mindset, with a mindful approach, if a person stops for a second to remind himself, this moment and again, over and over, every passage through a doorway can be an invitation for resting in the eternal presence. This is what the 613 *mitzvot* all boil down to: reminders to remember.

A Story

Rabbi Nosson Breslover was about to embark on a long journey to raise desperately needed funds for poor families. Just as the group he was to travel with was about to leave, he went over to the *mezuzah* and gently placed his hands on it. He told a member of the group, who was his student, that he needed five minutes for contemplation, and he asked the student to tell him when the time was up. He kept his hand on the *mezuzah* and rested his head on the doorpost. After five minutes, the student returned. Rabbi Nosson lifted his head and replied, "I am begging you give me a big five minutes, not a little five minutes." He explained that when a person kisses and acknowledges the *mezuzah* on his doorpost, he is asking God, "Even when I go outside, help me feel as if I'm still inside." "Inside" means real intimacy, real connection. "I need a long five minutes before I go outside, so I will remember to stay attached to God."

(Heard from Rav Moshe Weinberger)

A Reflection on Constant Awareness of Divine Presence

With respect to every religious action – Torah study, prayer, performing *mitzvot* – a person should accustom himself to say, "I am doing this for the sake of the unification of the Holy One, blessed is He, and His *Shechinah*, so as to provide spiritual satisfaction to the blessed Creator." He should accustom himself to utter this with the very core of his heart, and in the course of time he will sense a great radiance while saying it.

(Tzetel Hakatan 4)

A saying of the Baal Shem Tov (may his merit protect us) was based on the verse, "Lest you turn away [from God] and worship other gods" (Deuteronomy 11:16). At the moment that you allow your awareness to wander from the Holy One, it will immediately be as if you are worshipping other gods. This is the ultimate goal of understanding: to know that all of your powers and your very essence are from the Holy Creator – that He is the power, the capacity, and the force in all things, that He makes all things move, even you. When you let your mind wander from this thought, you become like an idolater, worshipping forces other than the Holy One, since you no longer hold fast to the thought that all of your power and essence are from the Holy One.

(Meor Einayim: Shemot, s.v. v'eileh Shemot)

Words of Light

Open your mouth and let your words illuminate.
(Berachot 22a)

THE STEREOTYPICAL VIEW of the silent psychologist nodding his head empathically while occasionally murmuring "um hums" is far from the typical scene during my sessions. I spend a lot of my time in session talking. While listening is central to my effectiveness, I'd say the main thing I do is talk. There is no magic, herbs or potions in this healing profession. Just talking and listening. In this drug obsessed pharmacological age, as bizarre as it may seem, these tools, when employed correctly, are consistently efficacious, sometimes miraculously so.

Talking and listening skillfully aren't skills reserved solely for mental health professionals. They help any soul seeking spirituality, solace and companionship. Long before Freud came up with his seminal discovery of analysis, King Solomon in Proverbs wrote, "Worry in the heart of a man lowers it down; but a good word makes it glad" (Proverbs 12:25). The Talmud (*Sanhedrin* 100b) transposes one of the letters in the word *yashchena* ("lowers it") changing it to *yisichena* ("speaks") emending the verse to read, "If a man has a worry in his heart, let him speak it out to others." Solomon's intention was to teach that through proper dialogue, a person's heavy heart can be lifted, restoring his spirit to health and equilibrium.

God created the world with His words, and He continues to maintain it with His words. At every second, He is whispering, "Let there be light. . . ." These words are the perpetual divine reality that dwells within the world and infuses life into every moment. The word of God is the perpetual divine reality that dwells within the

181

world and infuses life into every moment. God spoke, speaks, and is speaking perpetually to the world.

The Hebrew word *davar* means both "thing" and "word." Every "thing" expresses God's word within it. Man's purpose is to hear these words and express what he hears. In so doing, he reveals the essence of all things. A person can only gain that awareness with *da'at* ("knowledge"), the ability to connect to the present moment. With this awareness a person can't help but attend to the voice and speech of God that arises from within the creation. When man uses this unique refined ability of speech, he is able to reveal the essence of all things.

> Then the Lord God formed man of the dust of the ground, and breathed into his nostrils the breath of life; and man became a living soul. (Genesis 2:7)

What is the nature of the breath that God breathed into man? The biblical commentaries provide numerous interpretations of the quality of the breath that was breathed into man. Onkelos (who wrote the authoritative Aramaic translation of the Torah – which, according to tradition, was transmitted together with the written and oral Torah at Sinai) translates "living soul" as "a speaking spirit." God invested man with speech – the ability to "hear" God's speech and to express God's message in his own speech. This is a gift that elevates man above all other creatures. Thus, the Jewish philosophical teachings describe four strata of reality: *domem* ("inanimate objects"), *tzome'ach* ("vegetation"), *chai* ("animal kingdom") and *medaber* ("speaker"). The speaking spirit is the soul that lives within man, that which most distinguishes him from animals. Man's spirit is most profoundly expressed through the mouth, via the spirit of speech. "A living soul" is "a speaking being" because the distinctive characteristic of humanity is speech.

Being alive means being able to choose. Free choice simply means that a person has the freedom to choose. But a person never has the option not to choose. A person's speech is the epitome of this ability to choose, as speech is the most profound expression of the Godliness with which we are invested. Speech represents the ever-present reminder of the life-force infused into each creature by its Divine source. Speech is the defining characteristic of man.

The speaking spirit placed in man is the breath that God constantly breathes into him. It contains a person's ability to connect to the Divinity within as well as to that of each and every creature. Speech is not just talk, but rather a recognition of the internal and immersive Divine energy. Therefore, the speech to which I refer here is not only limited to the act of speaking and articulating external words (which, of course, is a manifestation of speech). Just as man serves as the connection between the higher spheres and the physical world, so too the power of speech, provides him with the ability to elevate the world to its spiritual source, cognizant of God's presence, or descend into a base, coarse existence. The spirit, the place of the emotion, of desire, is this connection point within man.

Adam was tasked with the job of naming all of the creatures in the Garden of Eden. The mystical writings teach that the name of an object expresses its inner, principal quality. Adam's ability to name objects meant that he possessed an understanding of the true meaning of all things. This power of understanding was entrusted to him because he was tasked with being the spokesman of, for and to all creation. (*Midrash Rabbah* 17:4)

The ultimate purpose for which man was created is not only to *listen* to, but to *hear*, the word of God that is contained in every object and to articulate it. That choice is ours to make as well: to hear and focus on the will of God that is in all things. We are able to be conscious at every moment of what is being *said* to us right now. "What is being spoken, told, whispered, screamed to me through this thing? What is this scenic view telling me? What is this tragic scene saying to me?" This awareness can only be accomplished through the attribute of *da'at*, the ability to connect to the present moment. Through unification with the present, each spoken word, when uttered or heard with *da'at*, or every thought with this awareness, manifests the vitality planted within man to uncover God's will and intent in all things. Words that are spoken with *da'at* are good words. That doesn't mean that these expressions are always easy to hear or melodic. But they are always constructive; they are words that build, or upon which one can build, filled with a sensitivity to what is transpiring precisely at that moment.

And I have put My words in thy mouth, and have covered thee in the shadow of My hand, that I may plant the heavens,

and lay the foundations of the earth, and say unto Zion: Thou
art My people.   (Isaiah 51:16)

God placed the power to plant the heavens and lay the foundations
of the earth in the speech He bestowed upon man. With our words,
what we say and how we lead our lives, we possess the ability to fix
or destroy both our own world and the worlds of those around us.
We have the power to lift our world, bringing about a unification
and fulfillment of the Divine will, or to debase our surroundings
with improper speech.

The speaking spirit, the breath that God constantly breathes into
us, constitutes our ability to connect to the Divinity within ourselves and within all creatures. What we say, what we don't say, and
the manner in which we express ourselves, all define our humanity
and shape our cosmos.

Cultivating the ability to hear the true message of existence means
that the power of speech has been refined to the point of perfection.
True speech is synonymous with the Godly, inner essence that exists
within man. With this speech comes the ability to tell ourselves and
everyone else of the extraordinary beauty in the world. To speak
and hear with *da'at* is to articulate the meaning and significance of
each and every moment. Whether it is a moment of intense joy or
extreme suffering, when articulated correctly, proper speech is the
perfect expression of God's will. If I use my speech correctly, if am
hearing correctly, I can become the spokesman of creation. I am able
to achieve a full partnership in the creation. That is prophecy.

"'And say to Zion, You are My nation.' Do not read 'My nation'
[*ami*], but rather 'with Me' [*imi*]" (*Zohar: Introduction*) – i.e., My
partner. "Just as I created heaven and earth with My words," says
God, "so do you possess the ability to create, build and sustain
worlds. Not only are you My nation, but you are elevated to actively
participate in this creative endeavor together with Me." God gives us
the ability to lift, repair and perfect all things with our words. Then
we can truly become like Him. Through refined speech, speech with
da'at, man, created in the image of God, can share in God's ability to
create and sustain worlds or effect the disastrous opposite. Through
speech, we have the ability to reveal how everything leads back to
the Ultimate source.

Is Ephraim a darling son unto Me? Is he a child that is dan-
dled? For as often as I speak of him, I do earnestly remember
him still; therefore My heart yearneth for him, I will surely
have compassion upon him, saith the Lord.

(Jeremiah 31:20)

The prophet is not making a statement in the name of God but
rather posing a question. Do I really have cause to love my son right
now? Is he a darling son, the child for whom I hoped and dreamed?
The reality of the situation is that Ephraim is far from this. The
nation of Israel, God's son, may be rebellious and rambunctious,
often discarding God's teachings and rebelling against his guidance.
Yet God, as it were, says, "No matter. Whenever I speak about him,
in spite of the difficulties, I cannot help but yearn for him, and
I grow filled with compassion and longing." God is not employing some form of autosuggestion or self-help mantra but rather
demonstrating how proper speech can remind each of us that the
Divine word resides within, and that we are tasked as the "speakers"
to expose the Divinity that has always been present – starting with
ourselves and then to the world around us. Jeremiah's prophecy and
direction is not indicating the creation of a new reality, but rather
the ever-present, truthful word in all things. Like all prophets, this
God-intoxicated man uses words to access Divine truth. That is why
all the prophets sound different, speaking as they do in their own
voices while channeling God's message. But, different as they are,
they all connect to God through carefully chosen and appropriate
words. We can do the same.

A Reflection on the Unity of All Creation

A Jew must always look at and focus on the intelligence of everything, and bind himself to the wisdom and inner intelligence that is to be found in each thing. This is in order that the intelligence in each thing may illuminate and enlighten him and his way so that he may become closer to the blessed *Hashem* by means of that thing.

(Rebbe Nachman of Breslov, *Likutei Moharan* I 1)

"In the entire Torah, as well as the entire world, for that matter, there is nothing but the endless light of the Infinite One, blessed be He, that is hidden and concealed within all things. This is how all the verses such as, 'There in no other but He,' 'The world is filled with His honor,' and 'I fill the heaven and earth' are to be understood literally: there is no act, utterance, or thought that does not contain the essence of Godliness, hidden and contracted within.

Therefore, when a person gazes and truly looks with his mind's eye at all of the things that pass in front of him, and sees their essence and vitality, and does not merely see their surface and superficial appearance, he will not see anything but the Divine power within them, which gives them their vitality, and brings them into being, and sustains them at each and every moment. *And a person who listens with intent to the inner voice which is within the material voice and sounds that his ears hear will not hear anything other than the voice of God that is at that moment enlivening and bringing into being that sound that he is hearing.*"

(*Hadrachot HaBesht* #1, appended to *Divrei Shmuel*)

Torah: The Sacred Now

TO EVERYTHING THERE IS A SEASON, and a time to every purpose, under heaven. (Ecclesiastes 3:1)

"To everything there is a season." There is a set season for everything that has and will transpire. The midrash on this verse comments, "There was a time for Adam to enter into Eden and a time for him to leave. There was a time for Noach to enter the ark and there was a time for him to leave. There was a time for Avraham to enter into the covenant. And there was a time for Abraham's children to be circumcised" (*Kohelet Rabbah* 3:1). This midrash clearly raises some very challenging issues regarding free choice and Divine omniscience. But without getting into these, the midrash's message is clear; a set season has been established from the beginning of creation for everything to happen.

Z'man, the Hebrew word for "season," refers to something in the realm of physical existence. Physical life and existence are bound by time. Created simultaneously, the two are inseparable. This midrash illustrates that everything in physical existence has a set time and place. The events in the lives of Adam, Noach, Avraham and all their future progeny, on some level, had been pre-ordained in the realm of physical life. However, the verse also mentions a "time for every purpose." That "time" isn't circumscribed by "to everything there is a season." Although transpiring in the physical world, it is not bound by the rules of physical existence. It is rather a singular event, a transcendent spiritual experience that could not be included in the general category of *z'man*: it is the giving and receiving of the Torah. Time out of time.

What category of time would the giving of the Torah fall into? The language of the verse reveals the unique characteristic of this unmatched event. The Hebrew word used here for "time," – *et* – is related to the word *atah* – "presently."

The conditions that were required for the giving of the Torah at Sinai are the same precise requirements for receiving the Torah subsequently; it must occur in the present moment. The present moment, which joins the past and the future, is not time. Right now, is rather the point between the past and the future. It does not occupy space and defies any measurement. The present moment steps out of time altogether. In order for time to be measured, it must have occurred. In the present moment, there is an infinite amount of time that can never be measured. Infinity is the absence of time, it could be said to be time-less, just as in the present moment. That moment can never be counted; therefore, it will and can exist infinitely, forever eluding the grasp of time. We exist in this infinite moment that is neither in the past nor in the future.

Jewish spiritual practice requires that we constantly seek to be aware of the Godly truth that imbues the present moment. Through the study of Torah, both the written and oral law, we are able to attach ourselves to God in every moment. The Torah which is transcendent, was and is given "*atah*," now, in the present moment. It exists in the continuous state of right now. It lives and breathes in just this moment.

When the will within God arose to create the world, He looked deeply into the Torah (*Zohar: Terumah* 161b). Therefore, everything has a root in the Torah. By studying it and following its directives, we awaken to an awareness of God's presence in all that exists.

The Torah and its commandments are a means of experiencing God, of seeing that there is nothing but God. That which is spiritual and transcendent, defies time. If a person wants to live in the realm of the spiritual, the world of the soul, he must live in the now. Everything that exists in the physical world is bound by constraints of time, either waiting to materialize or it is something that has already been and will be no more. Only the present moment is *chai v'kayam* – "alive and enduring."

In our limited, physical world, the Torah and the commandments that emerge from it serve as our connection to the spiritual essence of everything. They are our means of experiencing and responding to the presence of Divinity – God's enlivening presence that transcends time.

If we are fully present to what is happening right now, then every moment of life is calling out to us to focus on the "*atah*" and live and attach ourselves to the call of that particular moment. That is God speaking. In every moment of life, through all that we experience, see, feel, and do, we hear God's ever-present word. Every moment of my life where I am fully living in the present tense I am connecting to something higher, connecting with the transcendent. This requires being fully attuned to not just what you see and feel but requires keen listening and an open heart. To be with what is. And to see it for what it really is.

In the world of time, the sun rises and the sun sets, there are beginnings and endings, longing anticipation and fading memories. But the now, this very moment that we are in, is alive and vibrant. The passage of time cannot dim this awareness, and while the external physical façade corrodes and decays, the now is not subject to the things that occur within the realm of time. The now is always vibrant.

The whole world is filled with two different but parallel laments: the memory of "once upon a time" and the anticipation of "tomorrow will be better." These laments inescapably results in desolation. Time takes away what was and gives a false sense of what will be, but it doesn't give us now. On the contrary, dwelling on the lost past or unknowable future immobilizes you from action, paralyzing you into inertia. When a person attaches himself to the Torah that permeates existence and to the life that it infuses, he experiences a continuous state of now. This precious moment unifies and gives meaning to all the past and future. It is "a time for every purpose" (Ecclesiastes 3:1).

> Vanity of vanities, said Koheleth; vanity of vanities, all is vanity.
> What profit has man in all of his labor that he labors under the sun?
> I have seen all the works that are done under the sun; and, behold, all is vanity and a striving after wind.
> (Ecclesiastes 1:2, 3, 14)

King Solomon, the wisest of all men, studied man's actions "beneath the sun" – in the framework of time – and he saw that it is all vanity and futile striving. Man's time-bound sense of reality leads him to evil, distortion, lust and confusion. It can only end in disappointment. The striving after wind is the embodiment of the lust, distortion, confusion and obstruction that man pursues. All of these exist "beneath the sun" – the world that is measured by the dimension of time.

That is the world in which we are born and in which we will die. The world we inhabit is measured by moments and hours and days and years. Yet despite that, if we fully live in the presence, if we attach ourselves to the Torah of existence, we are able to rise and inhabit the world that transcends time.

> "And the tablets were the handiwork of G-d, and the writing was G-d's writing engraved on the tablets" (Exodus 32:16). Do not read *charut* ("engraved") but rather *cherut* ("freedom") for you will not find a freer person than one who is involved in the study of Torah. (*Pirkei Avot* 6:2)

A Reflection on Creation

"In the beginning" (Genesis 1:1). Rashi quotes Rav Yitzchak, who asked, "Would it not have made more sense for the Torah to begin with: 'This month is the first of months for you' (Exodus 12:2) – i.e., the sanctification of the new moon, the first commandment given to the children of Israel?" Rav Yitzchak answers by quoting the verse, "He declared to His people the power of His acts." (Psalms 111:6)

How does this explain the importance of the narratives of the Torah from "In the beginning" all the way until "This month"? While it is true that the primary purpose of the Torah is found in the commandments, which comprise the Written Torah, the Holy Blessed One also wanted to make clear that all of the Torah, indeed all of Creation, exists by virtue of the power of Torah: God looked in the Torah and then created the universe. This is the importance of the Oral Torah, which is ultimately dependent on our actions. That is, all of the stories of the forefathers are meant to show us how their very deeds became Torah. This is the meaning of the phrase, "the power of his acts"- the power that God placed in our deeds. That is the significance of the expression *ma'aseh Bereshit* (the act of Creation): the world came into being by means of God's ten utterances (therefore, Creation's very existence is contingent and dependent on Torah). *Our work in this world is to reveal that our every deed is sustained by this same vital force.* When, through our intention and awareness, all of our actions flow from a connection to this vital force of Torah, then we fulfill God's initial will, and in response, God renews the light of creation.

(Sefat Emet I 5, Bereshit 5631)

Raising the Sparks

T HEY TRIED TO KILL US. We survived. Let's eat!"
is a tongue-in-cheek summary of almost every "high-pro-
file" Jewish holiday. While eating or refraining from doing
so plays a major role in most contemplative traditions, the central
role that eating plays in Judaism is unique. In Judaism, eating is an
opportunity to effect a cosmic fixing of sorts, a rectification for man
and the world.

> So that He would make you know that man does not live
> by bread alone, but rather by whatever comes forth from the
> mouth of the Lord does man live.   (Deuteronomy 8:3)

People rarely eat solely out of the desire to quell hunger, just as people rarely enter therapy to treat an eating disorder that results solely
from an undernourished digestive system. All people must eat to
survive, but most people don't merely eat; rather, they relate to food
in either a healthy or harmful way. The act of eating has inspired
scholarly tomes and an even greater number of self-help books and
resources to discuss our complicated and often dysfunctional relationship with food and its consumption. It is no coincidence that
the Hebrew word for "bread," *lechem*, is associated with the word
for "war," *milchamah*. Every time a person sits down to eat, he has
entered a battleground of sorts, where an inevitable confrontation
awaits. That confrontation is an evocation of the first battle, the first
trial, and the first defeat. In fact, all of our defeats with that last piece
of layer cake can be traced to this breakdown. Eating from the Tree
of Knowledge of Good and Evil was not a simple violation of the
diet God prescribed. Ironically enough, the eating itself wasn't the

problem. As already discussed, the root of Adam and Chava's failure was their removal of the fruit from the tree, their desire to experience pleasure separate from its source. This is the root of all of our own subsequent failings as well. It is this eating disorder, the eating without *yishuv hada'at*, from which all existential angst derives. The removal of God from the sense pleasure of this world is the loss of paradise that occurs with each bite. Precisely when Adam and Chava believed that God's eyes were no longer constantly fixed upon them, they became susceptible to the sin in the garden and all future rebellions against God's will. But theirs was not a sin of eating. It was a sin of forgetting. Their error was one of intention, not appetite.

The potential corrective action of eating is our endeavor to return to the state of man before the sin, man's ultimate return to paradise. Of course, there can only be one way to correct this error. When eating is sanctified, it reattaches the fruit to the tree. This rectification does not occur solely in the realm of eating, but eating is the "battleground" where the implementation of that rectification is often most pronounced. This makes each meal a ripe opportunity for a person to foster his abilities to rectify this dislocation in all the other areas of his life.

The earth and all that fills it belong to God.   (Psalms 24:1)

The heavens are the heavens of God, but the earth He gave to
man.   (Psalms 115:16)

"So which one is it?" asks the Talmud. Does the earth belong to God, or did He give it to man? In typical Talmudic fashion, the answer is that in fact both verses are true. One verse refers to the condition before a person recites a blessing over a piece of food, when it still belongs to God. After he recites the blessing, it belongs to man.

What exactly transpires with the recitation of the blessing? Imagine holding a red, delicious, juicy apple in your hand. And before you instinctively take a large chunk out of it, you pause. You stop and reflect. "Where is this urge to eat coming from? Where did this apple originate? How does it feel and smell? How wondrous are the processes of chewing, of swallowing, the thousands of taste buds and the olfactory neurons stimulated without any thought or effort, the marvel of the seamless efficiency of the enzymes and the digestive system and their ability to extract nutrients from the food, while simultaneously removing the excess!" This thought process must inevitably result in the elevation of a purely animal activity to a spiritual and intellectual one. The blessing serves to bring one's attention to all of these phenomena, and more. A mindful blessing contains the remedy for the mindless reenactment of the first sin and thereby elevates that act of eating to an act of *tiqun* – "repair" and perfection.

In truth, the land will always belong to God. But we can gain a share of it when we acknowledge the Divinity within. Reciting a blessing with awareness that we are benefiting from God's benevolence and creation, allows us to acquire in the most tangible way what the world is really about. The blessing is that acknowledgement. It is the sacred pause consecrating the most physical of acts with Divinity.

God greatly desires a dwelling place in the realm of the physical, and gave the earth to man for the sole purpose of revealing His dominion. This revelation is the basis of our relationship with God. When engaging in the physical, we must not automatically detach ourselves from God. To the contrary, with our blessing we acknowledge that our mundane physical needs are intimately connected to our Godly inner essence. God gave the earth to us so that, as we engage in the physical, we do not detach ourselves from Him but, on the contrary, we consecrate our acts. Each bite becomes an affirmation of faith, but only if we consciously act to sanctify it.

It might be hard to ignore the little voice in your head whispering, "What are you talking to your apple for? Doesn't that seem just a little crazy?" Ours is a culture where, far too often, if we see something and we want it enough, we consume it. It's simple. It's efficient. And it is mindless. It is the true poison of the snake. When a person stops and holds the apple in his hand, looking at it or maybe even gently closing his eyes, in that precise moment, he is tasked with the choice of saying "This is mine" or "This is ours." He is acknowledging and remembering that the world and everything in it was created by and sustained through God's word; that in everything there is a holy spark that sustains it. Furthermore, he is confronting the sobering and inspiring reality that God did it . . . for him. By reciting a blessing over the food that he eats, a person declares that it is not just the food but also our physical appetites, which are gifts of the Creator as well. He created the apple. He created our ability to taste and enjoy it. "Taste and see that the Lord is good; happy is the man that takes refuge in him" (Psalms 34:9). Just as with every breath, person and moment, every kind of food exists as it does because of the unique permutation of Divine speech and letters which form to make every bite unique, each being and moment are a distinct and new expression of the Divine will.

When a person's recitation of a blessing generates that awareness in him, the holy spark that is contained within the food can once again be reunited with its source, uniting with man's own essential being. With this presence and acknowledgement, then, and only then, does a person have the ability to fully enjoy this morsel, to nourish both his body and soul. If he were to be ascetic, his body would suffer, and if he would eat without a blessing, his soul would wither. But together the two join to correct the sin of mankind. Every blessing that is recited is a means of seeing the world correctly. The fruit has once again been re-attached to the tree, as we have been re-attached to our creator.

> A land that the Lord, your God, looks after; the eyes of the Lord your God are always upon it, from the beginning of the year to the end of the year. (Deuteronomy 11:12)

There is a geographical location in which the presence of God's watchful eyes can be felt more than in any other location – the holy land, the land of Israel. Only in that unique location can the Torah be fulfilled completely. Israel is where, almost paradoxically, we are tasked to live in a physical world, working and toiling in its soil, and only through physical labor and activities can we fully reveal Godliness. When our awareness of God becomes so clear, then everything, no matter how banal or mundane the activity, becomes a conduit for connection. Unlike Egypt, where water came from the Nile and could simply be redirected to irrigate the soil, the land of Israel requires rain from the heavens, because God wants us to pray for it.

This is the true beauty of the land of Israel. Israel's beauty is not merely in the aesthetic quality of its scenery and vistas. Rather, it possesses beauty by virtue of its being the land that God's eyes are constantly watching, literally filled with the eyes of God. While there can be no place void of God, the Torah is emphatic that the land of Israel is the only place in the world that has His gaze on it perpetually.

There, it is possible to perceive the world through God's eyes. It is therefore the land of prophecy. The Hebrew word for prophet is *navi*, from the root word *niv*, which the prophet Isaiah uses in the expression *niv sefatayim*, "the product of the lips" (Isaiah, 57:9). The highest form of speech is prophecy, because it uniquely stems from the ability to correctly and fully articulate what one is seeing and feeling. By seeing and speaking the truth of what we see, we demonstrate our repair of the first sin. When a person knows and contemplates this, he is able to connect to the unique aspect of the land of Israel, the aspect of having God's eyes on him always. By reciting a blessing on the food we are about to eat, the food we eat transforms to produce of the land of Israel. This doesn't mean that the orange in your hand is magically turned into a Jaffa orange, but, rather that, the blessing serves to bring about this awareness, the eyes of God, into the food you are about to consume. Even if a person is exiled, far away from the beauty of the land of Israel, if he is able to stop and properly recite a blessing, then what he is doing at the moment is seeing the world for what it really is: God's world. No matter the time and place you find yourself, you can taste the beauty of the land of Israel. The mouth that says, "Blessed are You," is no longer far away from the Promised Land. He has not been transported magically to the land of Israel, but rather holds the land of Israel in his hands. "The earth He gave to man" is a specific reference to the land of Israel, so when that blessing is recited at that moment, the land is being given to a person no matter where he is. Whether he is standing in Miami, New Orleans, London or Belfast, in that place so far physically from the land of Israel, he is reminded that the land of God was eternally given as a legacy to him as a Jew. To bless means that a person looks at the world in the right way. His blessing is an acknowledgement of the deeper truth of what he sees.

This concept applies equally in every area of our lives, including those physical activities that do not require the recitation of a blessing. But it is clearest in the act of eating. Our lives and sustenance come directly from God's ever-constant providence. When we are aware of this, every bite can be filled with the land flowing with milk and honey, and we can attain a taste of the world-to-come.

A Reflection on Spiritual Nourishment

And they saw God and they ate and drank.

(Exodus 24:12)

So too, a person who reflects on these matters, will note the natural processes by which the nourishment received by the body is apportioned to every one of its parts. These evidences of wisdom observed by a person will stir him to thank his Creator and praise Him for them. As David said, "All my bones shall cry out: O God, who is like You" (Psalms 35:10). Thus, the food passes into the stomach through a tube that is utterly straight, without bend or twist. This tube is called the esophagus. The stomach grinds the food more thoroughly than the teeth had already done. Then the nutriment is carried into the liver through fine intermediate veins which connect these two organs (bile ducts), and serve as a strainer for the food, permitting nothing coarse to pass through to the liver. The liver metabolizes the nutrient it receives into the blood, which distributes it throughout the body, sending the vital fluid to all parts of the body through conduits formed for this purpose, resembling water-pipes. The waste substances that are left are eliminated through canals specifically adapted to that purpose. What belongs to the green gall goes to the gall bladder. What belongs to the black gall goes to the milt (spleen); other substances and fluids are sent to the lungs. The refuse of the blood passes into the bladder.

Reflect, my brother, on the wisdom of the Creator manifested in the formation of your body: how He set those organs in their right places to receive the waste substances, so that they should not spread in the body and cause it to become sick.

(Rabbi Bachya ibn Pakuda,
The Duties of the Heart:
Gate of Discernment, Chapter 5)

Likewise, when eating, bear in mind that the taste and sweetness of the food are derived from the vitalizing force and sweetness of Above, and that this constitutes their vitality. Inorganic matter too has a vital force, as is evident from the fact that it has existence and durability. It follows, then, that the Divine vitality from Above is to be found everywhere.

(*Tzava'at HaRivash* 90)

Becoming Jacob's Ladder

IN THE COURSE OF OUR LIVES there will often come a point where each of us will ask the questions below, or some version of them. For some, the question will be so shattering that the seeming impossibility of arriving at a satisfactory response will shake them to their core, leaving them broken or disillusioned. Others will gloss over it, never daring to consider it for more than a few moments before moving on. And there are others – like you and me – who will live with it on a constant basis, struggling and grasping for solutions, at times feeling some sense of equilibrium but more often than not perplexed. No one is immune from it. Make no mistake: this questioning should not be seen as some unfortunate, regrettable occurrence. This is precisely the challenge we are tasked with. It is our purpose and duty to ask these questions. And the quality and meaning of our lives hinges on our ability to approach and answer these questions successfully.

> And he dreamed, and behold a ladder set up on the earth, and
> the top of it reached to heaven; and behold the angels of God
> were ascending and descending on it.　　　(Genesis 28:12)

The world we experience is filled with conflicts and contradictions. It is a world of polarizing opposites and painful extremes. These opposites cause a person to question the order and meaning of the nature of this world and the benevolence of an omniscient Creator. Light and darkness, joy and suffering, birth and death, good and evil – the list is endless, and it confronts us on a daily basis. Can there be any order to the chaos with which we are confronted on a perpetual basis? Is there a purpose to existence, to my existence? Is there an answer to the endless "Why?" Does it all make sense? Can we impose some sense on it?

Names are used both to define and to create a relationship with the named object. But if the named object is unknowable and beyond estimation, then whatever name is used is inherently inadequate. You can never count to infinity. God in His essence is unknowable. Even the name used colloquially for God, *Hashem*, just means "the name." That is because we are unable to really know God. Rather, the names we use as a device to describe or to call to Him reveal more about us than about Him; We call Him names that reflect how we perceive Him in our relationship with Him and how the Divine appears to manifest through its revelation to us.

In the story of creation, God is introduced to us with the name *Elokim*, reflecting mastery. This is because the definition of *Elokim*, as explained by the commentators (and this is the intention a person should have when reading or saying this name), is that God is the Master of all of the distinct and disparate forces within creation.

There is no greater contradiction, no greater dissonance, to the absolute unity and oneness of God than the separateness of this finite world. If God encompasses all, how can God (or we) be separate? The first letter of Creation, the Hebrew letter *bet*, is the second letter of the Hebrew alphabet. The number two does not only connote more than one. The number two connotes division and strife, divergence and discord. Anything more than unity brings with it confusion and doubt.

The creation of a world made up of day and night, light and dark, ocean and dry land, heaven and earth, and all its inherent and ensuing contradictions, had to emanate from the name *Elokim*. And because of all of these confusing contradictions, most of the ancient world began to believe and think that maybe there was more than one God! Maybe there are different gods for different tasks. Dualism, Gnosticism, and polytheism had to be the only way to make sense of it all: "There has to be a separate god for every disparity in my life." If I pray to the sun, or the clouds, or the trees, perhaps they will bless my crops."

"I am the master of all," *Elokim* says, "all of these seemingly disparate things." The multiplicity is not in God, but rather in the fact that He is the Master of all of these disparate forces. Only by His mastery, may everything appear unified. For the world to be created and its on-going existence, the name *Elokim* must be manifest, because within the name *Elokim* itself (the name being plural) is that which allows for and even accommodates the illusion that there is duality. It therefore had to be the name of Creation, because it is the name that allows for free choice. (Even in *gematria*, the traditional Jewish system of assigning numerical value to each Hebrew letter, the name *Elokim* equals 86, equal to the numerical value of *hateva*, which is "nature.") *Elokim* equals the world of nature, responsible for all the conflicting, separate things in nature that would have us imagine and believe that there are different gods and different forces.

The difficulties and questions we have in our lives all stem from the inability to balance the perpetual conflict and differences that we see with our eyes. The physical world we see is the world of *Elokim*. The name *Elokim*, therefore, connotes free choice and reward and punishment. It can also be synonymous with judgment and strength. Even the Hebrew word for "judge" is derived from this attribute, because it is the point of judgment from which to make sense of all of the conflicts surrounding us, to find the truth amidst opposing variations.

But there is another, concurrent way that God runs the world, through an entirely different name – through the name of *Havayah*. This name, comprised of the Hebrew letters *yud-hey-vav* and *hey*, the Tetragrammaton, is also known as the Ineffable Name. It is not uttered or spoken. Its correct pronunciation is both forgotten and forbidden. This name combines past, present, and future, and represents that God was, is, and will be. The Hebrew letters of this name are able to make up the words *hayah* ("was"), *hoveh* ("is"), and *yihiyeh* ("will be"). Thus, this name represents that God was, is, and will be. It is the name of *Havayah*, the name of just being, unbound by the limits of time. This name represents the Infinite Transcendence, extending from everything that was, through everything that will be. It stands in stark opposition to *Elokim*, whose plurality connotes dualism, in that *Havayah* connotes absolute unity.

When you and I look at the world, our immediate impression is only of *Elokim*, the name that is in control of all of the conflicting forces, a world whose garments appear to be continuously changing. Now it is night, and now it is day. Now it is light, and now it is dark – the appearance and presence of constant change. This is the God who created and manifests himself *in* nature. But there is also, equally and ever-present, the immutable name of *Havayah- Yud-Hey-Vav* and *Hey*, the presence of He Who was, is and will always be – who transcends nature. The instinctive feeling of conflict I feel when I look with proper perspective at the world where *Elokim* reigns is balanced by the transcendent yet immanent name of *Havayah* that fills and unifies this world of light and dark, of good and evil. Beyond that place of conflict, the name of *Havayah* tells me that there is a presence of God that never changes and is never altered.

> For I the Lord change not; and you, the sons of Jacob, you
> have not perished.   (*Malachi* 3:6)

"I – the Ineffable Name, *Yud-Hey-Vav* and *Hey* – will not, do not, and cannot change. I am and have never changed. Before, during and after, I am the same *Yud-Hey-Vav* and *Hey*. There is nothing else. I am *Yud-Hey-Vav* and *Hey*. There is nothing else."

Man created in God's image is the closest approximation we have to the "real thing." If God is somehow revealed in this world, in these two seemingly contradictory ways, through the name *Elokim* and the name of *Havayah*, this revelation must also somehow play out in our own lives. When a person looks all around him and, more importantly, when a person begins to look at himself, he can't help but see the raging conflict. There is so much inconsistency around us, but, more painfully, within us, where the dissonance is often overwhelming. But God makes a promise to each and every one of us. Just as, in the world, only *Elokim* can be perceived on the surface and *Havaya* is hidden almost imperceptibly away, so too our immutable nature flows perpetually, like an underlying current, beneath our chaotic surface and nature. We all have the same immutable nature in spite of our external turmoil. Just as all of the external garb of the cosmos does not alter the essential nature of the world, so too the essential nature of the self, the soul, is immutable. "I have never changed," says God, "and neither have you." In the same way, underneath all of the apparent disparity and contradictions and conflicts that exist in the world, there exists the guarantee that "you, the sons of Jacob, you have not perished." The immutable soul is connected to the reality of God's existence in the world.

The verse's usage of the name Jacob is not incidental. After Jacob awakens from his legendary dream, immortalized by the name,

Jacob's ladder, he declares, "How full of awe is this place" (Genesis 28:17). Having seen a ladder whose head touches the skies and whose bottom remains rooted on the earth, as all the while angels are climbing both up and down, Jacob cannot help but exclaim in amazement. He understands with all that has already happened and that which is yet to transpire, that there is, at least, at the core, a unifying reality that encompasses all.

It is with the realization of this remarkable vision that Jacob makes an oath. "And Jacob vowed a vow, saying: 'If God will be with me, and will keep me in this way that I go, and will give me bread to eat, and clothing to put on, so that I come back to my father's house in peace, then shall the Lord be my God" (Genesis 28:20–21). *Yud-Hey-Vav* and *Hey* will be my *Elokim*. There will be a connection between the Ineffable Name and the name *Elokim*, between immanence and transcendence.

Through his dream, Jacob realized that he himself, as well as his progeny, were to be the ladder that joins the lower world to the higher world. Jacob experienced himself as both the top and bottom of the ladder, along with ascending and descending spiritual forces. They were all part of one vision. This vision tells Jacob that this world has conflicts, ascents and descents. One part of the ladder is rising to the heavens and the other is descending to the deepest depths. And Jacob himself is the ladder, the connection between heaven and earth, the ability to be the conduit and conductor of these disparate energies. And we are the sons of Jacob, *Bnei Yisrael*, not of Abraham or Isaac, but of Jacob, the embodiment of the unity of the universe, whose other name, Yisrael, means struggle, endurance, and ultimately victory.

In spite of our inner fragmentation, of our being individuals who are lost within themselves, Jacob's promise is that he will seek to embody a life where *Yud-Hey-Vav* and *Hey* is *Elokim*. In the world of *Elokim*, amidst all of those differences and confusion, one can still be attached to the Source of all things, the world of *Yud-Hey-Vav* and *Hey*, which never changes. There is no need for any desperation because "there is a perfect part within me. Ultimately, I will be brought back to my true self – which was, is and will be." Every Jew was, is and will be forever.

As the children of Jacob, we have the ability, no matter what, to say "*Yud-Hey-Vav* and *Hey* is *Elokim*" (Deuteronomy 4:39). In a world where the name *Elokim* seems so dominant, with its multi-plicity of opposing forces, there is still only *Yud-Hey-Vav* and *Hey*. In a world where a perfunctory glance would indicate that there is no God, there is still only *Yud-Hey-Vav* and *Hey*. We have the power to be the ladder to see that this too is also *Havayah*. We too can connect the opposites. There can always be a permanent connection between the outer manifestation of God's external trappings and the inner dynamic that is the source of all creation, a bond between these two names of "what I see" and "what I believe," a bond in the indestructible nature of the soul, irrespective and in spite of what may have transpired.

> The Lord of hosts is with us; the God of Jacob is our high
> tower. Selah.   (Psalms 46:11)

God is the master of the legions and hosts who rule and is even the source of opposite forces. God unifies all of them. As such he is called the God of Jacob. Abraham, who personified loving-kindness, and Isaac, who was the pillar of strict judgment, could not be described as unifying forces. These two extremes stand at the opposite ends of the spectrum of service of the Divine. But Jacob is the bridge, the ladder that holds these attributes together. In the Kabbalistic works, Jacob is described as personifying the attributes of splendor, truth and harmony. He can fuse the opposites of the loving-kindness of his grandfather Abraham and his father Isaac's fiery judgment. The ability to contain the two opposite, conflicting emotions of love and fear, and make sense of the opposites and bring them together in a healthy integrative way, is the power of the attribute of Jacob, the final of the triad of our nation's forefathers. The rabbis teach that the number "one" is a representation of absolute unity, "two" is division and strife, and "three" signifies a median point between opposite and mutually defining terms, which brings unity back to the original schism. Our task in this world is to make unity out of disunity.

The verse in which God creates harmony out of a universe that is filled with conflicting forces refers to him in the role of "God of Jacob." For good reason. Only when it is clear that God brings (and contains) all opposites together, only then can He be called the God of Jacob.

How full of awe is this place! (Genesis 28:17)

We live in a world defined by the name *Elokim*, the name used to create a separation, a veil that creates a distortion in how we perceive things, which allows the world to have free choice. When a person stands in the presence of this mystery, he is confronted with an overwhelming paradox: on the one hand, the multiplicity of existence symbolized through the name *Elokim*, while on the other hand the name *Havayah* telling him that there is only a unifying oneness. *Havayah* was, is, and always will be immutable. There has never been, nor will there ever be, a change. When a person is cognizant that he stands in the presence of complete something and complete nothing, he is overcome with a sense of wonder. Just like Jacob before us, all we can do is exclaim, "How awesome is this place." (Parenthetically, this is the source of the sanctity of the Temple, *sha'ar hashamayim*, "the gate of heaven," to earth, from mundane to Divine. It was a place of opposites, a place physical in its stones, wood and sand, yet utterly suffused with Godliness.) In a sense, each of us is a model sanctuary, an infinite soul confined in finite flesh.

Although on the surface there is a multitude of opposites, beneath the surface and apparent contradictions of a world of *Elokim* there is the wonder of body and soul, the wondrous presence of "For I *Hashem* [*Yud-Hey-Vav* and *Hey*], I have not changed, and you, children of Jacob, I have not destroyed." (Malachi 3:6)

Unfortunately, although not too surprisingly, in this world of confusion in our relationship to God, others and especially ourselves, there is a perpetual shifting and spiraling of ups and downs continuously fluctuating between closeness and distance, running forth and returning. Our entire lives vacillating between ongoing tension between two movements, a constant tension between love and fear, dark and light. But beneath this conflict we have the ability to access an underlying constant truth. Despair and frustration come if, even just for a moment, a person takes all the differences he sees in the world as being the definitive story. That world is true, but it is not the only truth. Beneath the apparent conflict there is the name of *Havayah* that is completely engraved on the soul of every Jew, who is a portion of the living God. The cacophony of dissonance is ultimately accepted when a person understands that ultimately, it is a part of a Divine harmony.

A Reflection on God's Immanence

Whatever a person's place, that is the place where he must entreat God. The place where he stands – "where he is there" (Genesis 21:17) – he must elevate this place and connect it with the One who transcends place. This is God, who is the "Place of the world." Then this person can serve God in truth. There is no place that can prevent Him. Through sin, you can fall to the "place that is not good" – to the lowest, grossest, filthiest place. Even there, remember God. For He is the "Place of the world." In Him, there is place for all. Therefore there is no such thing as a fall. In all the places where a person is driven, he can still return to God. "And from there you shall seek the Lord your God" (Deuteronomy 4:29). From there! From the place where "He is there."

Man's activity is bounded by space and time. It is here that the forces of the other side have their hold. But God himself is beyond space and time, in a realm where there is only good. Here the forces of the other side have no hold at all. Here everything is sweetened. "If I ascend to Heaven there You are . . . The days were formed but the One is not among them" (Psalms 139: 8, 16). It follows that there is no place or time to which we can try to flee from God. Despair is totally ruled out. The reason is that all places in the world are close to God. Beyond all places, He gives life to them all. He sustains all the places and all the levels in the entire creation. The same is true in the case of time, so in every place and in every time, we can find God. Place and time are both included in Him. They are only emanations of God. And by returning to God, we ourselves can transcend place and time. (*Likutey Halakhot; Tzitzit* 3:9, 15)

A Practice

Sit comfortably where you won't be disturbed. Take a few slow, deep breaths. Breathe in deeply and then, as you exhale, relax your body. Let go of whatever tension you can.

"Let everything that breathes praise God." With your every exhalation, your breath goes from below to above. Then, when you inhale, it returns to you from above. In this way, the Divine part within you unites with its source.

With each inhalation, gently note the name *Elokim*, and with each exhalation gently note the name *Havayah*. Allow your breath to serve as a vehicle to help you identify all of the powers in the world with their Source (cf. *Likutim Yikarim*, p. 15b).

Teshuvah: The Return to Impermanence

THE SOURCE OF ALL OUR JOY comes from one thing: being. It is the root of repentance – *teshuvah* (literally "return"), returning to that place where one stands and simply is, returning to the root of one's identity. It is precisely for this reason that the holiday of Sukkot, the festival of joy, follows immediately after the penance of Yom Kippur, the Day of Atonement. Atonement resulted from a process of intense self-scrutiny and introspection, but, at its core, ultimately resulted from the realization of the deep, unbreakable connection we have with God. The days following this atonement are filled with the joy that emerges from the felt presence of that deep connection. The flow of such a powerful, intimate closeness, is not static but rather one where the change inherent in every moment is palpable. Everything is changing constantly. But, instead of the feelings of loss that typically accompany change, there is a feeling of joy and tranquility, because of the realization that everything is impermanent except for this unbreakable bond.

When the weight of sin has been lifted off our shoulders with the absolution of Yom Kippur, we find ourselves covered within the temporary dwelling hut, the *sukkah,* a symbolic representation of our feelings of being encompassed by the wings of the Divine Presence. On Yom Kippur, we come to the root of our identity, to that place where there is no guilt or shame, and all of the ugliness has been shed, revealing our true selves. "The place upon which you stand is holy soil" (Exodus 3:5). To arrive at the realization that the place where you stand, wherever it is, is holy, is also infused with the Divine presence. This is the realization for which we strive. The place we inhabit is holy; for we are holy. A person no longer requires something outside of the "I," desiring things that are outside the realm of himself, who he truly is. But this liberating attitude requires cognizance, the *yishuv hada'at*, that place and time are not fixed or permanent, and that this impermanence is the soil of being. It is life itself with the non-guarantee of anything but its temporality. The people we love will not live forever, and this next breath could be our last. And that is precisely the basis for the cultivation of *simchah*. It's not the joy of winning the lottery, but the refreshing clarity that comes with the knowledge of our essential goodness in the present moment, regardless of what came before and regardless of what might follow.

Real change is possible, and it's right here in this moment. All of my limiting beliefs and hardwired tendencies are no longer the stone fortresses I once believed them to be. The *sukkah* therefore must be a temporary dwelling, representing the person I was for so long and am no more. The love and closeness we feel is so exciting, but we can only dwell in it for a moment, because there is something novel forthcoming. The unbending clouds in my life that seemed so fixed and permanent, with the belief that what existed a moment ago, must persist and exist a moment from now, has dissipated. This impermanence is what allows for constant growth, the belief in change, the soaring to new heights of whatever will be, will be.

This is a taste of the age of messiah. People tend to believe that the messiah's arrival will be accompanied with stability and the certainty we all spend so much time craving in vain, because this world by definition, is unstable. How many of us squander opportunities and chances in order to ensure that we never feel that we are on shaky ground? Rather than bring terra firma, the messianic age will bring with it spiritual instability.

The word "instability" typically connotes something that is not optimal; nothing could be further from the truth in this instance. The holiest stability one can achieve is to be constantly in flux and unstable, living today, right now, not for the now but in the now. The messianic age will be a time period marked by constant fluctuation and the instability of dwelling in the temporary abode of the moment. When everything will be temporary, nothing will feel old. Nothing will get stale. Nothing will feel stuck anymore.

The Kabbalistic works describe how in messianic times women will be able to give birth every day. (I have not yet shared this with my wife.) This (clearly) metaphorical statement alludes to the consciousness that will pervade society. Every moment will be akin to a new life, entirely original and fresh. Life, for the most part, will not be very different from our current state right now, other than the fact that everyone will possess this awareness. Everything will be acknowledged as temporary, and this liberating knowledge will pervade our consciousness: everything new, never being trapped, never being stuck.

> May He, the Compassionate One, erect for us the *sukkah* of David, which has fallen.   (Grace after Meals)

This was the life of King David. His entire life was a *sukkah*, a temporary structure enveloped in the awareness of the Divine Presence. At each moment he was a new person.

A midrash tells that God showed Adam all of the coming generations. When Adam saw that David was destined to die in childbirth, he asked God: "Master of the world, is there no repair for this?" God replied: "So is it My intention." Adam then inquired: "How many years will I live?" God told him: "A thousand years." Adam asked, "Is there such a thing as a gift in the heavens?" To which God answered: "Yes." Adam said: "Let seventy years of my life go towards him."

Destined to die in childbirth, David had his life extended by 70 years. Those years were spent living with the knowledge that he was subsisting quite literally on "borrowed time." Perhaps this imbued him with the awareness that every moment of his life was temporary and, therefore, where each breath was another gift.

This is the challenge and the reward of living with *yishuv hada'at*. Anytime we get stuck in our ideas of how things are or should be, we have built a facade of a permanent dwelling. We seek and crave stability and the means to ensure it. But there is no permanence. Life ebbs and flows. King David teaches a new way, the path of the master of *teshuvah*, the ability to collapse into now, where the constant unfolding of the present moment is simultaneously accompanied by the recognition that at every moment I can change; I can become new.

This mindset is brought to the fore during the ceremony of *Kiddush Levanah*, the sanctification of the new moon. With its waxing and waning, the moon is the symbol of renewal and perpetual motion. Even in the darkest of nights the moon is poised, waiting, slated to ultimately reveal itself once again. During *Kiddush Levanah*, some have the custom to greet one's neighbor with the traditional phrase, *Shalom Aleichem*, "peace be unto you," as though one had never seen him before (even though you've been standing next to this person for the past few minutes). It's likely you have known the person you are greeting for your entire life. But during the ceremony of renewal, you are reminded that right now, at this moment in time, you are seeing this person for the very first time. This neighbor that you knew a minute ago is not the neighbor you know now, just as the person you believed yourself to be a minute ago, is not the same person who you are right now.

Following that, one recites the verse, "David, King of Israel, is alive and enduring," that is to say, never dying. Never dying. Alive and enduring is an oxymoron, for all things that live are destined to die. But David's life teaches us how our lives can be different. His life was the life of a *sukkah*, where every second is alive with the liberating awareness of impermanence. In the totality of this moment there is no death. Now you are alive. Each now is forever.

> Return us to You, O Lord, that we may be restored! Renew our days as of old. (*Lamentations* 5:21)

> And now, O Israel, what does *Hashem* your God demand of you? Only this: to fear *Hashem* your God. (Deuteronomy 10:12)

> The sages teach: The phrase, "and now," connotes a moment of *teshuvah*. (*Bereishit Rabbah* 21:6)

But how is it possible for *teshuvah* to work? Everyone knows that what's done is done. And yet we ask God to "restore our days as of old."

The Hasidic masters explain: "Each and every Jew must believe with complete trust that at every moment he is revived and sustained by the blessed Creator. As the rabbis expound on the verse, 'Let every soul praise God' [Psalms 150:6]: Praise God with every breath you take [*Bereishit Rabbah* 14]. At each moment, the Divine life force desires to leave the body, and at every moment God returns it to a person with renewed vigor." (*Kedushat Levi: Eichah*)

Teshuvah, "return," is accessible to *everyone*. A person does *teshuvah* with the implicit belief that he is a renewed life force, a new creation. On that basis, his earlier transgressions are not recalled. But if he does not believe in this – that he is created anew at every moment – *teshuvah* cannot avail; and its invigorating power will not be accessible to him.

This explains the midrash that "and now" means *teshuvah*. When a person believes that he is made into a new being at every second, right now, then and *only* then, can teshuvah be effective. "Return us to You, O Lord, that we may be returned!" We return through our belief in God's ability to "renew our days as of old" (*Kedushat Levi*: *Eichah*).

Our tendency to cling to a finite world that gives the appearance of an independent, fixed reality, is the source of all our sorrows. It is the impediment to meaningful return. Every moment is a new revelation of God's presence. But the cognitive knowledge of this is not sufficient; we need to cultivate the awareness that each new moment of existence for every single creature emanates directly from God. This is the foundation of all Divine service. It is the foundation of *teshuvah*. It is David's *sukkah*. It is the *sukkah* of this moment.

A Reflection on Impermanence

And the living creatures ran and returned as the appearance of
a flash of lightning.   (Ezekiel 1:14)

"Running and returning" is the pattern of the breath, the life
force of the soul, the "breath-soul." Through breath meditation, a person can connect with the life force that is being
offered to him in the most intimate and caring of ways. For
this reason, the rabbis teach, "Praise God with every breath
you take."   (*Bereishit Rabbah* 14:9)

A person must always be aware that from moment to moment
the blessed Creator with great kindness and mercy instills in
us a new vital force. From moment to moment, the blessed
Creator renews our very being. This is what the rabbis meant
when they said, regarding the verse, "Let every soul praise
God," that at each moment the breath seeks to leave us, and
the Holy One, in great mercy, watches over us from moment
to moment and has compassion on us, and does not let the
breath depart. When a person maintains this awareness, he is
perpetually being recreated, time and time again. This generates a fervor and passion in his service of the blessed Creator,
since everything that is new or renewed is filled with passion
and zeal. And since we are all recreated at every moment, we
can possess enthusiasm perpetually in the service of the holy
Creator.   (*Kedushat Levi: Nachamu*)

When the Rebbe was involved in his devotions, everything
he did required great toil and effort. No form of devotion
came easily, and the Rebbe literally had to lay down his life
in many cases. Everything required tremendous effort, and
he had to work hard each time he wanted to do something to
serve God. He fell a thousand times, but each time he picked
himself up and served God anew. The Rebbe became accus-
tomed to constantly begin anew. Whenever he fell from his
particular level, he did not give up. He would simply say, "I

will begin anew. I will act as if I am just beginning to devote myself to God, and this is the very first time."

This happened time and time again, and each time he would start all over again. He would often begin anew many times in a single day, for even in the course of a day there were many times when he would fall away from his high level of devotion. But each time he would start again, no matter how many times that happened, even within a single day.

(Shevachey HaRan, #5, 6)

A Story

The two famous brothers, the holy Rabbis Elimelech of Lizhensk and Zushe of Anipoli, would often impose exile upon themselves, in order to share in the pain of the exiled Divine Presence. They would pose as simple beggars and mingle with the common folk to learn from their experiences.

Once, while they were traveling with a group of ruffians, some of the members of the group were accused of being thieves, and the entire company was thrown into jail. The brothers humbly accepted this as the decree from heaven and resigned themselves to their predicament.

As the afternoon progressed, Reb Zushe began to sob.

"Why are you crying, brother?" asked Reb Elimelech. "Surely you know that we will have a swift and speedy salvation from this prison cell."

"I am confident that we will be redeemed soon," replied Rabbi Zusha. "But the time for the afternoon prayers is drawing to a close, and" – gesturing to the bucket that served as the cell's toilet – "because it is forbidden to pray in the presence of excrement, I am unable to pray."

Rabbi Elimelech placed his hands on his brother's shoulder and told him gently, "True, you cannot pray now because the law forbids it. But why weep? You know that the same God who commanded you to pray also commanded you not to pray when the room is unfit for prayer. By not praying in this room, you have achieved a connection with God. While it might not be the connection that you had initially sought, if you truly want the Divine connection, here is the opportunity that God has presented for you at this moment to obey His law, no matter how it presents itself."

Rabbi Zushe exclaimed, "My brother, you are right!" Energized by his brother's words, he banished his feelings of dejection. He grabbed his brother's arm and began to dance with joy. Soon, the entire cell, filled with the dregs of society, joined in the fervor, dancing and singing with the joy that the euphoric brothers were spreading.

Hearing the commotion, the guards came running. One guard pulled aside one of the inmates and asked him for the cause of the commotion. "I'm not sure," answered the prisoner. "All I know is that those two Jews were discussing the pail in the corner when they began to dance, and we all joined in."

"Is that right?" scoffed the guards. "They're ecstatic because of the pail, are they? Remove the pail from the cell!" he cried out. The pail was promptly removed. And the brothers began their preparations for the afternoon prayers.

(Heard from Rav Moshe Weinberger)

A Prayer

My God,
The soul that You placed within me is pure.
You created it, You fashioned it, You breathed it into me,
You safeguard it within me, and You will eventually take it from
me
And restore it to me in the time to come.
All the time that the soul is within me,
I give thanks before You,
Havayah,
My God and the God of my forefathers,
Master of all works,
Lord of all souls.
Blessed are You God
Who restores souls to the bodies of the dead.

PART IV: Shabbat
A Day of *Yishuv HaDa'at*

The Sanctity of Being

Let each man remain in his place. Let no man go out of his place on the seventh day.   (Exodus 16:29)

W HEN I DESCRIBE the act of letting go to my clients, I have them clench their fists tightly for a few seconds, concentrate on that sensation, and then contrast the feeling with sensations experienced upon releasing their tight grip. I then ask them to relay to me what that experience was like. Very often, they articulate feelings of relief and relaxation. Deciding to let things be and accept them as they are might be the most difficult choice a person will ever make. That is because most people view "letting go" as connoting apathy and indifference (and even giving up). But that couldn't be further from the truth. On the contrary, "letting go" is an active process. It is the radical acceptance that one must not only accept that things are as they are but that one must *permit* things to be as they are. When a person is able to radically accept things as they are, he can truly experience freedom.

> I have a great gift that I have in my storehouse; its name is Shabbat, and I wish to give it to Israel. Go and explain it to them.   (*Shabbat* 10b)

Shabbat, the Jewish Sabbath, is *the* primary tool to achieve *yishuv hada'at*. It is *yishuv hada'at* realized. It is the ultimate expression of "letting go," of non-doing and acceptance, of looking at life with a complete willingness to see things as they are, deeply and truthfully.

The constant tension and movement of this world engenders an unspoken feeling that something is not quite right, promoting a sense of instability. A life of *lech lecha*, in which a person is driven to perform and produce, connotes that something is missing. One is always striving, moving towards, always incomplete. This restless attitude describes the six days of the week. We quell this emptiness by immersing ourselves in our work – the 39 types of activity necessary to build the tabernacle and civilization.

Shabbat is the antithesis of that which is not Shabbat, all the busy motion and uncertainty, all the doubt and insecurity, all the striving and becoming. It is not merely doing nothing but rather an imperative for not doing. A person's ability to stand still is the epitome of Shabbat, *the* gift of Shabbat. A gift is something, not nothing. Shabbat is not a void. It is a completion in which a person can feel whole, peaceful, and at rest.

Our rabbis teach that a person must enter into Shabbat with the mindset that *all* of his work has been completed. To someone who has never tasted the sweetness of Shabbat, this may appear to be unrealistic and quixotic, especially on a weekly basis, knowing that Sunday is around the corner. A job may not yet be done, a meeting may have ended with unresolved issues, or a building project might be far from complete. But Shabbat is the ability to look at the unfinished business deal, the as-yet incomplete construction project, and still feel complete. They are all at the moment where they should be. There is nothing lacking in the palace of the King. On Shabbat, a person can experience the serenity that comes with having all of his work completed, the stillness that is intrinsically linked with everything being exactly the way it is supposed to be. Planning and working are part of the six days of the week. That includes a person's spiritual work as well: his self-help projects and striving to be better. Everything is now as it is supposed to be.

With Shabbat, a person resides in *chochmah*, a deep understanding of the condition of the world and of himself. He lets go of the details and gives himself over to the realization that God is running the world. Shabbat is the source from which the person, the week, and the entire world draw their blessings.

Standing still is the personification of the "fear of God" – not in the trembling and frightened sense, but in the sense of awe and wonder. The root of the Hebrew word for "awe," *yir'ah*, may also be translated as "to see." Shabbat is the embodiment of our corrected vision, of our ability to see the world as it truly is: as the domain of the One. The stillness of Shabbat enables us to cultivate an awareness that everything (including oneself) is in its right place.

A curious exchange recorded in the midrash between the great sage Rabbi Akiva and the Roman magistrate Turnus Rufus can help us understand how to cultivate this attitude of "being" on Shabbat. (Rabbi Akiva was often challenged by Turnus Rufus, an accomplished philosopher, to debate theological and philosophical issues. These debates, although simply worded, are filled with complexity and depth.)

Turnus Rufus asked, "If God honors the Sabbath, why doesn't He keep the wind from blowing, the rain from falling, and the grass from growing on Shabbat?" Rabbi Akiva replied, "If two people share a courtyard, they are not permitted to carry in it unless they both contribute to an *eruv*. But if it is only one person, he has free rein over the entire yard. The same is true of God: since there is no other authority beside Him and the entire world is His, He has free rein over the entire world" (*Midrash Rabbah, Bereishit* 11:6).

Turnus Rufus asks a very straightforward question of Rabbi Akiva: How can God require you to keep Shabbat when He himself apparently violates Shabbat?

To understand Rabbi Akiva's answer, we need a certain amount of background information. Carrying or transferring an object between a public domain such as a street (a *reshut harabim*) and an enclosed private domain such as a courtyard (a *reshut hayachid*) is biblically prohibited on Shabbat.

There is also a domain that is technically private but, because it functions like a public domain (for example, a courtyard shared by several residents), it is liable to a rabbinical prohibition of transferring and carrying. In order to circumvent this rabbinical prohibition and make carrying and transferring permissible, an *eruv* must be created. The *eruv* integrates separate properties into one shared domain.

The requirement to create an *eruv* is only relevant when numerous individuals share a courtyard. If there is only one owner and no other residents, the entire discussion is moot. The owner would certainly be permitted to carry wherever he wanted to, because this is his private domicile, a *reshut hayachid*. That was the scenario that Rabbi Akiva referenced in his response to Turnus Rufus.

Our eyes deceive us into believing that the world around us

consists of many separate domains. In fact, from our limited and delusional perspective, each individual believes himself to be master of his own domain. Our illusion of control, mastery, and freedom, opposes and seemingly contradicts the presence of God in our lives as the true master of the universe. Shabbat reminds us that there is only the *reshut hayachid*, the domain of the One.

"How is it that God transports winds on Shabbat?" asks Turnus Rufus. Rabbi Akiva answers that He may do so because Shabbat is the day when the world reverts to its truest form: to God's private domain. Like the sole owner of a courtyard, God can carry anywhere He wants. In our minds, bringing a wind from the Pacific Rim to Miami Beach constitutes quite the journey. But for God, it is one courtyard. It is all His domicile.

When we sanctify ourselves and our awareness, we access the revelation of the reality that this world is actually a private domicile and not the open, public domain it appears to be. Once a person settles into this consciousness with his mind, body and soul, feeling in his very being that there is no other intrusive presence claiming sovereignty, that there is no sharing with anyone or anything else other than the Divine, he can tap into this private domain and assume his role in a unified, tranquil, orderly universe. All of the turbulence and competing forces are illusion. It is the domain of the transcending unity.

During the six days of the week, that reality is unclear. At that time, we perform acts that belong to the 39 categories of work forbidden on the Sabbath. These are creative activities we engage in to exercise control over our environment. During the six days, we are charged with the obligations of creative labor. On Shabbat, just as God rested at the end of Creation, we too rest, aware that we are in the private domain of the Creator. There is nothing more to do.

As noted above, rest is not merely a cessation of activity; it is not a void. Rest is an active commitment to a positive acceptance of the world as it exists. The world of the six days of the week, in which the 39 categories of labor are dominant, can often confuse us, due to its constant movement and activity, which creates the appearance of unlimited diversity and diversions. Moreover, it suggests that only through activity can we bring about change. The myriad voices and noises emanating from the public domain pull and push at our psyches so that we cannot experience *yishuv hada'at*. And so we feel that we can never stop. And the outgrowth of this frantic movement is the spurious, damaging belief that the essential purpose of this world is indeed all the doing, coming and going that characterize and animate the six days of the week.

> Let each man remain in his place. Let no man go out of his
> place on the seventh day.   (Exodus16:29)

The purpose of Creation is that we will somehow arrive at the conclusion – despite living in a world of separation and division, a world that appears to comprise so many seemingly different domains –that there is only one private domain: the domain of the One. As all things centrifugally drift further and further away from the root and source of existence, Shabbat counteracts the negative attraction of the public domain and reveals the innermost current flow through everything, bringing everything to the center.

Shabbat is a mandate to lift our eyes and see everything to the root of its existence, to feel the immanence of God that enlivens all of existence, to see that everything is all part of one bigger picture. Shabbat serves as the reminder that the only way a Jew can achieve *yishuv hada'at* is by living in the felt presence of the domain of the One, the Transcendent Unity. The only way to do this is to shift from our "doing" mode to a "being" mode. This is the practice of Shabbat.

This state of knowledge goes beyond the physical senses. On Shabbat, we can ascend from the level of choosing to the level of knowing. The six days of the week represent an existence of choosing: of deciding, distinguishing and judging. In the course of our busy day-to-day lives, our minds are a steady stream of wanting and not wanting, liking and disliking. The constant flow of judgment and striving are emblematic of the mundane week. Shabbat, however, creates the mindset that while we may not understand each detail, we are able to know, because we are connected to what truly is right now. That is our connection with the higher unity, the domain of the One.

On Shabbat, we can savor a reality higher than that of a life based solely on the effects of the choices that we have made; Shabbat allows for a glimpse into an existence that is greater than our decisions of good and bad, right and wrong. It provides access to a supernal awareness that intuitively knows of our inherent connection with our Creator. We feel no need to tell God how much we do for Him or to remind Him how much He cares about us; we simply experience the essential connection.

During the week, our minds are tormented by doubt. These questions are the primary labor of the six days of the week. Shabbat resolves all doubts, because it confers the knowing, the security that we can transcend the world of doubt. It is the ability to look at the world with Divine eyes. Shabbat allows us to rest knowing that all things are in the private domain of the Master of the world.

A person who does this experiences a foretaste of the Messianic period, a time "that is entirely Shabbat and rest for life everlasting" (Shabbat Addendum to the Grace after Meals). While we must and should continue to engage with the world that surrounds us with its many domains spinning in an apparent attempt to disconnect from its source, for, until the Messiah arrives, we are tasked to toil in this world of concealment. God in His grace provides a blueprint for us to gain access to the private domain that is truly the gift of being, the gift of Shabbat. And that feeling, that awareness, can inform the rest of our lives, for once you have experienced the Divine, it becomes a permanent part of you.

In My Place

> As they are united above in One, so she is unified below in
> the mystery of One, to correspond to them above.
>
> *(Zohar, Terumah)*

---

*C*HILLUL, AS YOU REMEMBER, means an empty
space, specifically something that was once full and is now
stripped of what it once contained. Anytime a person loses
his consciousness and forgets the Divine Presence that imbues the
current moment, he gets pulled away from the private domain and
into the public domain. When a person is no longer living with the
awareness that there is only one real domain, he is taking a world
saturated with Godliness and emptying it of the presence of God.
Chillul Hashem means not believing in and trusting in that presence. Whenever a person transgresses one of the laws of the Torah,
by definition renouncing the authority of God, he experiences the
automatic and concomitant element of *chillul Hashem*.

But, notwithstanding the broad nature of *chillul Hashem*, only
one transgression is permanently identified with the word *chillul*
in all of Jewish literature. And that is the violation of Shabbat. To
be *michallel Shabbat*, is customarily translated as "desecrating the
Shabbat" but literally means "rendering the Shabbat vacant," strip-
ping it of its substance. Although every sin is a *chillul Hashem*, there
is something unique about Shabbat that prompts this description
of the consequences of its violation. All of the Torah's laws emanate
from God, but only Shabbat is his gift, his queen, his precious bride.

"Let each man remain in his place" (Exodus 16:29). Wherever a
Jew dwells, his place is referred to as "sitting beneath the yoke of
heaven." Our constant and consistent awareness of God's presence

guides our actions, much like a yoke guides the ox. With this clarity, we can occupy our place with certainty and conviction. But very often, we can get mixed up with lies that result from the Tree of Knowledge of Good and Evil – the tree of doubt. The perpetual and confusing motion and upheaval of the six days of the week loosen our footing. This unsteadiness is compounded by our apparent failings and feelings of emptiness. Then the stability we once had is slowly replaced by a feeling of being adrift, trapped in the mire of physical existence. Everywhere we look, it seems that something other than God is acting. Worse still, not only does our place seem completely bereft of God, but it seems antithetical to His presence.

Shabbat reveals that everything is enlivened and animated by the presence of God. Shabbat provides us with the ability to feel this presence. On Shabbat, God's monarchy is revealed. Then, wherever we are in the world, in that place, we are able to be there utterly and completely united with the felt presence of God. Everything in the world reverts to Him. "He is the Place of the world, but the world is not His place" (*Bereishit Rabbah* 68:9). The cultivation of this mindset settles our racing minds and worrying hearts.

On Shabbat, every Jew can feel settled in the place in which he finds himself. There is no need to go anywhere, nor any need to do anything. The commandments that restrict physical movement on Shabbat were given to help us cultivate this mentality. The prohibition against going too far from one's place is a direct corollary of the realization that a person must see himself being exactly where he is and where he needs to be. During the week, this awareness might be opaque, but on Shabbat a person can sit and simply be with the felt sensation of God's presence. "Don't strive. There is nothing more to do. There is nowhere to go. There is just being with the transcendent unity."

That is why *chillul* exists especially in the realm of Shabbat. The whole purpose of Shabbat is to reveal that we are living in one courtyard and that God is the Place of the whole world. *And so, on the day that God rested from creative labor, we are commanded to emulate His ways and just be.* If a person ignores this mandate, he has created a *chillul Shabbat.* That means that this infraction, more than any other, causes the vacating of the state of being in the presence of God.

A careful analysis of the laws of Shabbat underscores this point. Most people, when exposed to Shabbat for the first time, feel overwhelmed by the succession of Don'ts: "Don't carry. Don't go outside the boundaries. Don't light a fire. Don't drive. Don't answer the phone." This can feel restrictive and even petty. However, when one internalizes the realization that the prohibitions are designed to reinstate a mindset of rest from certain types of creative labor, in effect shifting our perspective to Shabbat mode, then "don't do" becomes an invitation to "just be." The restrictions are a constant reminder that sensitize us to what really is and help us reside in the domain of being. Traveling from one place to another distant place is forbidden on Shabbat, even though doing so does not create anything, because on Shabbat we are tasked to embrace and recognize a reality where there is nothing more to do and no other place to be.

This is the *yishuv hada'at* that Shabbat offers. It is the antidote to the confusion of the world. Even when we do not focus on the clamor of the world, on the crowded streets of Times Square, we feel pulled in a million different directions, because residing within us is our very own internal public thoroughfare. During the week, we may feel pulled in 39 different directions by our drives and desires. Stillness – refraining and withdrawing from the public domain – constitutes the greatest antidote to the difficulties, confusions and burdens of the six days of the week. Shabbat is the anchor that gives us a secure place, tethering us to the Divine.

Nothing exemplifies the "being" aspect of Shabbat more than the fact that it has no active commandment. True, there is the rabbinic mandate to mark the arrival of Shabbat by lighting candles and reciting *Kiddush*, and to mark its departure by performing the *havdalah* ceremony, but there is no ceremonial marker on Shabbat itself. Shabbat is "sitting and not doing." Shabbat is "sitting and being."

To be sure, a taste or memory, or semblance of this awareness can be felt whenever a person brings his attention to this reality. Indeed, as best we can, we are supposed to bring Shabbat awareness into the six days of the week, by using them to remember and prepare for Shabbat; thus, we can provide them as well with vitality and sustenance. But until the end of days – a "day that is entirely Shabbat" – we can only fully taste this experience on Shabbat.

God says, "Make Me a sanctuary, and I will dwell in them" (Exodus 25:8). Note that God is not saying that He will dwell within the sanctuary, but that He will dwell "in them" – in each and every one of us. Shabbat is a "sanctuary in time." On Shabbat, we have the capacity to rest in the domain of being. Any time a person does not get lost in the public domain but retains his God-consciousness, he is remembering the Sabbath. To guard the Sabbath and keep it holy requires our acceptance of the presence of God right here and right now.

The most favorable time of the week for a person to access this consciousness is from the time Shabbat begins until the moment it ends. Since the creation of the world and every Shabbat thereafter, the gift of Shabbat is an opening into a state in which a person lives with the constant consciousness of God's presence. Because of this reality, Shabbat requires that a person's every action and every word be imbued with this awareness. If a person pulls a leaf off a branch, walks where he shouldn't or turns on a light, he has lost that God consciousness, creating a vacuum, a *chillul Shabbat*. That doesn't mean that a person must sit paralyzed in a dark room for the period of Shabbat. Rather, he should remain attentive and aware that, when he is not cultivating this awareness for even one second, *chillul Shabbat* can occur. The whole foundation of Shabbat is to feel and embody this at every moment. The whole day is one of constant remembering and awareness. It is a day of reminding ourselves at every moment to rest in the presence of Shabbat, cultivating a constant awareness of that presence.

A person's heart can then become sanctified as a living abode, a sanctuary, for the *Shechinah*. Until the physical sanctuary is rebuilt, the *Shechinah* resides within each of us, in the heart of each Jew. A Jew who lives in the domain of the One is transformed into a sanctuary, imbued by and living in the presence of God.

Most importantly, the existence of the Shabbat in this world, and the manner in which it is capable of transporting us to a level of communion with the Divine, illustrates the basic message of this book: that there is no distinction between the bliss of the next world and our experience in this world, if we can but channel our perceptions and awareness appropriately.

Remember the Shabbat Day:
Keep it Holy

THERE ARE TWO POWERFUL FORCES that are ever-present, and which, although often constructive, can become a source of desolation.

The first of these is inertia – not in the way modern physics uses this word, but more along the lines of statistical probability. There is a certain monotony and humdrum quality in our daily lives to which we become inured. The sun rises in the east and sets in the west. The farmer plants and sows and harvests. There is cold in the winter and heat in the summer. "To everything there is a season. . . ." And so it goes: the circle of life.

This consistency and familiarity allows us to go through life with a sense of security. This predictability, often taken for granted, is crucial to our emotional survival. We feel threatened when we feel that we have lost our stability. In the event of a trauma, God forbid, the loss of predictability proves to be the most debilitating factor, psychologically and emotionally. All of the safety and order that were presumed to be part of everyday living are revealed to have been only a façade.

However, this comfort of day-to-day life may come at a steep cost, because it can impart the impression that things do not change and are not susceptible to change, resulting in a feeling that we are trapped in an immutable and uniform cycle of life. This can take away one's belief in the power of renewal, in new beginnings, in the hope of starting again. A person who feels this way about any negative circumstance in his life – "I'm alone, I'm unemployed, I'm addicted . . ." – is prone to feel that the exact same set of circumstances will exist tomorrow as well. If the forces of the universe have conspired to work against him until now, why should tomorrow be any different? These thoughts can form the beginning of a depressive mindset. The inevitable result of this belief is that a person feels stuck.

The second force, which is connected to the first, is the feeling of servitude, of being subordinate and insignificant. Contemplating that we are just a speck in this massive universe could serve to humble us so that we recognize that we are part of something much greater than ourselves. This realization, applied correctly, can provide perspective and a sense of duty. But more often, thinking in this way results in our feeling that we lack all control and that what we do doesn't really matter. It seems that the rules of the universe are immutable and certainly do not offer any hope that we have the power to effect the change that we are looking to bring about in ourselves. We are enslaved to circumstances – to the traffic light, to our boss's demands, to our upbringing, to our genetic makeup – to an extent that we are powerless to change, to become, or to improve.

In response, the Torah provides two reasons for the observance of Shabbat: one, in order to recall that God created the world (Exodus 20:7), and two, in order to remember that God took us out of Egypt (Deuteronomy 5:11). Those two reasons provide a response to the two above-mentioned forces that inhibit and hinder growth in our lives. They do so by imbuing us with the one value cherished above all others: freedom. Shabbat is the path to liberation.

First, when we bear in mind that God created the world and re-creates it on a constant and consistent basis, we are made aware of the possibility of our own renewal. Bearing in mind the creation reminds us to live our lives in a way that defies monotony and statistical probability, a creative life in which we acknowledge our own role in the creation and revelation of God's glory in this world. We gain an awareness that gives us the capacity to accept, oppose, or confront a life of doing that seems to drag on interminably.

Shabbat comes bearing its message: "Enough! Stop! Then you may start again." It is a reminder built into every week that we all have the ability to start again. Shabbat calls to us to remember creation: "Remember that you were created and realize that you can always begin again, just as it was 'in the beginning' when the spirit of God hovered over the chaos. You are not stuck in some endless quagmire." The ultimate renewal is simply to be. Paradoxically, as it might seem, we are able to change the direction of our lives simply by standing still. Without Shabbat, there is no life. There is only an imitation of life.

Secondly, Shabbat helps us remember the Exodus from Egypt. This was not a one-time occurrence. We are constantly tasked to realize that we leave Egypt every day. Shabbat is our prompt to remind ourselves that we are now slaves to no man, and that we must free ourselves on a constant and continuous basis. We must not be slaves to technology or any illicit drives or desires, or the temporary escape of drugs, alcohol, or other palliatives. If we are not sensitive, if we are not aware, then we can become mired in our wants and never once pause to embrace life as it is. Shabbat is our beacon, our ever-present reminder, that truly nothing can enslave us. The opinions of the world cannot dictate what we will do, nor can they define our values and priorities. Our desires cannot compel us to act in a way that violates our value system.

We are constantly led about by our cravings, which pull us in all sorts of conflicting directions. Doing something you later regret simply because you weren't able to sit for a moment and consider the ramifications of that action is the result of feeling enslaved, feeling out of control, too trapped to break the cycle.

Shabbat comes along and screams, "Be free!" One day a week a person can taste something of the world-to-come. The 39 labors forbidden on Shabbat that shackle a person to the illusions and delusions of the six days of the week can be shattered.

From an "outsider's" skewed vantage point, this idea of liberation couldn't be further from the truth. For him, Shabbat doesn't come to liberate a person but to enslave him. With its myriad restrictions, how can Shabbat be a day of freedom when the rest of the world is free to do whatever it wants? Shouldn't a day of rest be one in which we can do whatever we want, a day of unfettered license?

When a person states, "I am a Sabbath observer," he is often met with a look of pity, as though he had confessed to a decree of confinement or prison sentence. Not being able to go anywhere you want, or do anything you desire, doesn't sound very attractive and certainly doesn't sound very much like freedom. This person can't do anything! Is there anyone more deserving of sympathy? From the outside looking in, it looks as if on Shabbat everything is "no." Those with outside eyes who have not yet experienced the liberation of Shabbat, who have not yet felt Shabbat from the inside, cannot understand that Shabbat is the ultimate expression of freedom. But for those who are inside, saying "no" to everything external and distracting, is a way of saying "yes" to one's true self. Those who have experienced shifting from the mode of doing to the mode of being, of being themselves and being in the felt presence of the Creator, can only describe this experience with one word: freedom.

> A rest of love and magnanimity, a rest of truth and faith, a rest of peace and serenity and tranquility and security, a perfect rest in which You find favor. May Your children recognize and know that from You comes their rest, and through their rest, they will sanctify Your Name.   (Shabbat Prayer)

Appendix

Hashkatah
The Subject of Quieting [the Mind]: A Practice

The source of the following meditation is Rabbi Kalonymus Kalman Shapira, the Piaseszner Rebbe, also known as "the Rebbe of the Warsaw Ghetto," who was murdered by the Nazis. This text was not transcribed by the Rebbe himself but rather was taught by the Rebbe and recorded by one of his students.

Whereas most Jewish mystical works shy away from describing meditations and practices, the Rebbe offered practical techniques to come to a state of *dveykus* ("clinging" or "attachment" to God) and enlightened consciousness.

(The translation of the text is in bold followed by my comments.)

Comment of the transcriber [a student of the Rebbe]: Woe for that which has been lost, for I do not remember the entire discourse. But that which I do remember I write here as a remembrance.

The Admor (an abbreviation of the honorific "our lordship, teacher, and Rabbi"), of blessed memory, began at that time with the statement of our Sages (*Berachot* 57b) that "a dream is a sixtieth part of prophecy." That which blocks a person from an influx from above is his sense of self.

We seek to remove the blockage of which the Admor speaks. In order to do so, we must loosen or let go of the sense of self, move on from ego to acceptance of what is, and open oneself to the presence of the Divine. If we are full of ourselves, there is no room for anyone or anything else. Being full of ourselves implies that there is no space for anything else. All movement and transformation are caught in a logjam of ego and delusion. But if we are open, accepting, and empty, we can ameliorate the ways in which we are holding onto the self, and that allows for the possibility for transformation.

The greatest obstacle to sensing the closeness and awareness of God is the ego, man's own presence.

As the verse states, "I stood between the Lord and you at that time, to declare unto you the word of the Lord" (Deuteronomy 5:5). It is the "I" that stands between man and God, the presence of one's self, the detached feeling of "I." The presence of a person's self-blocks, diminishes and ultimately overwhelms his ability to feel God's presence.

Because of that, if a person's self-centered, automatic thoughts and feelings are awake and reactive, it is difficult for the presence of God to enter into him from the higher world.

A person's mind is preoccupied. Something has taken up space in his mind. His mind is filled with the sense of himself, with the "I." There is no room to allow for the presence of God in his mind and heart.

However, when a person is "asleep" and his thoughts are quiet, then, because he can no longer be preoccupied with his own thoughts of self, he may be able to have some presence of God in his mind and heart.

This is possible because there is no self- directed consciousness that had previously existed and served as a barrier to Divine inspiration. Letting go of the self isn't an intellectual process, but a process that goes beyond the flow of thoughts to a place of bare perception – of pure seeing and being. When we avoid getting caught up in the flow of thoughts, and simply observe what is actually happening in this moment, then something opens up, something present that is both beautiful and vibrant. It is existence. It is creation. It is Divinity.

This is what the Talmud is alluding to. When a person is sleeping, he cannot be fixated on his desires, so there is more access to Divine inspiration – something akin to prophecy, an experience of complete God-consciousness.

The principle objective, therefore, is to reach that objective while you are awake: to be able, while you are awake, to come to that state of being asleep.

The Rebbe is not referring to a mindless state like daydreaming. Rather, while you are awake, come to a state of "sleep": that is, quiet your mind of the thoughts and desires that flood into a person constantly, ceaselessly. The essential technique and goal is to cultivate this sleep state (which is pure awareness) while awake, as much as possible.

When a person reaches this state, he quiets his thoughts and desires, which flow in a person without end. This "sleep" consciousness is the quieting of both components of a person's thoughts and desires.

These two processes are fundamental parts of ourselves that block us from Divinity: our mind's barrage of thoughts and our endless flow of desires. A person pays attention to the constant flow of his thoughts, to the onslaught of ideas, images, fantasies and stories, which give us no genuine peace and prevent us from being present to what truly is. Paradoxically, our minds are too busy to accomplish anything. Similarly, if we observe our desires, there is a constant flow of wanting one thing and not wanting another, of being upset at the occurrence of something we don't want to happen and then being gratified when something we do want happens. And of course, whatever we are feeling only lasts for a few moments, and then something else arises in its place. In this state of constant bombardment there is never genuine peace. There is no quiet or deep joy and satisfaction. We are unable to truly be present with the Divine Presence.

So the practice is to create space that is free and open, and not trapped by the flow of thoughts and desire. Thought and desire are not the enemy. This is a practice of quieting, not obliterating, of allowing oneself to simply take a step back and mindfully observe these phenomena so that we are no longer trapped by their flow and prevalence.

This is the way of thinking. This is the way of a thought; one thought leads to another thought. One thought becomes entrenched and entangled and becomes a web of thoughts. It is extremely difficult for a person to escape that. So you get stuck in this whole web of thoughts and wants. If a person would look

at his thoughts objectively, thoughts that are popping into his head – just for one day to just simply observe one's thoughts – he would find that there is no difference between his thoughts and an individual suffering from psychosis. The only difference is that the person (who is psychotic) is someone who believes those thoughts or is compelled to do things based on them. But the thoughts themselves are no different. [In the words of the transcriber . . .] He then gave us concrete advice about this quieting.

The point of *hashkatah* meditation *is to observe your thoughts.* Anyone who has spent any time observing his mind (something that is difficult and requires training) will notice an incredible level of foolishness and absurdity. Thoughts that he would never expect, bizarre ego-dystonic views and ludicrous scenarios are constantly being produced, *because that is what the mind does.* Our minds churn out one crazy thought after another. Simply by noticing this without judgment, we can approach these previously taboo thoughts with humility and detachment.

How can a person allow for God's presence to enter into his consciousness while he is in the middle of a flood of movies in his brain all day long? What room exists for God so long as a person is so preoccupied with a million thoughts running amok? How can he feel the presence of God?

Typically, a person thinks but is never cognizant that he is thinking. He thinks about everything but the thinking process. A person begins the practice of quieting his thoughts by spending a few moments focused on observing what he is thinking right now.

[In the words of the transcriber . . .] He [the Rebbe] said first that one simply watches for a set period of time, observing his thoughts. Then a person begins to feel that his mind is emptying out. Paying attention to what he is thinking helps prevent a new rush of thoughts from rushing into his mind.

By being less caught up in the flow of thought and intellect, by simply observing rather than engaging with the thought (which only serves to give the thinking more energy and continue the process of entangling the person in one thought or another) a person slowly clears a space in which the flow of his thoughts slows down. The moment a person is not as entangled or identifying with the productions of his mind, a space for his soul is created, where he can observe these phenomena. This is *not* analyzing and deliberating about one's thoughts but rather a process of observing them, just as a person would observe a physical experience. In doing this, a person takes the first step to recognizing that he is not his thoughts.

Most individuals have the misinformed belief that their thoughts constitute the most genuine parts of their nature. The Rebbe demonstrates that they are not. In fact, they block a person from realizing and accessing his authentic nature because they possess a cloudy, incessantly entangling quality. The fact that a person can observe his thoughts clearly demonstrates that he is not his thoughts, because there is some other part of himself, some part of his awareness, which now observes that part of himself that is his thought. That is the meaning of the Rebbe's reference to the erasure of the "self" – not the true observing self, but the self whom a person so readily and mistakenly identifies himself with – i.e., the thoughts that he assumes to be a component of his essential self and the most clear indicator of his identity, but which are in fact nothing more than passing sensations.

The second component of this practice, of working with the self, is a person's detached, nonjudgmental observation of his thoughts. This is a witness consciousness, in which a person does not judge or get involved, but just observes the experience of his mind. In so doing, he removes the fuel that feeds a misappropriated sense of self. He steps back from the constant mode of production of thought. He attains the ability to experience Shabbat even in the middle of the week. He observes the constant flow and change, the arising and departing, of his thought. For the Divine to enter, we need to pause.

And then a person can begin to recite a verse, such as "The Lord is the true God" (*Jeremiah* 10:10).

He recites this like a mantra, over and over, in order to focus his mind, which is now calmed from customary distractions. Repetition is a very effective tool for strengthening this consciousness and enabling single minded focus to emerge. The Rebbe explains that the most powerful way to focus is by reviewing and repeating something over and over again.

The verse connects your head – which is emptied of thoughts, a mind that is free – to one thought of holiness.

After a person has quieted his mind and opened up a space that holiness can permeate, he observes his inner, holy experience of consciousness, and from that observation, he moves to cultivating that experience.

A person attaches his mind to just one thought of holiness. Then he can begin to make requests of God. He can call out to God for spiritual matters that he needs: strengthening his faith, nurturing his love and awe of God, and so forth.

Through this quieting, a person puts himself in a situation in which his mind is open rather than closed, in which his soul is focused rather than scattered, and he can be genuinely affected.

At that time, I [the transcriber] was privileged to hear from the Rebbe a way of using this technique of quieting the mind in order to strengthen faith. And these are the Rebbe's words.

"I believe with complete faith that the only thing above is *Hashem*, and there is no reality outside of *Hashem*, and everything that I see in the world around me is just an illumination of *Hashem*."

And he [the Rebbe] repeated this over and over a number of times. But he advised that a person not say this strongly and forcefully, because the entire purpose is to quiet the mind. And so it should be said softly. If a person were to say this too strongly it would only serve to awaken his ego. So he should rather do so in a gentle tone. Similarly for the love of God (and the following are the words he used): "There is nothing I want more than to be close to the holy Creator. There is nothing I want more than to feel His closeness." This technique can be used to rectify all negative character traits. But that it is done in a positive way, by emphasizing the opposite of the negative characteristic. If a person has been afflicted with the character trait of laziness, the approach is not to speak about avoiding laziness or how not to be lazy (with the focus on the negative) but rather about acquiring zealousness and alacrity.

This isn't about rejection or pushing away, but involves embracing everything and being open to everything, and then cultivating useful qualities to deepen one's connection with the Divine. Pushing things away just serves to strengthen them.

We see this with a child. When a person sees a child crying, he doesn't say, "Don't cry," because that guarantees that the child will cry even more. He [the Rebbe] taught that it is also possible to attain quiet by watching the small hand of a watch, which barely moves at all, for a set period of time. This, too, has the effect of curbing the impulses and thoughts.

After this quieting, which has the effect of bringing in a Divine influx, he [the Rebbe] instructed us to say the verse, "Show me, God, Your path," using his special tune. How awesome, wondrous and pleasant was that experience that I [the transcriber] was privileged to see in the merit of my friend.

The Rebbe stressed the importance of this matter. And he spoke on this at length in the context of developing faith, so that after a few weeks of using this method, when a person says "This is my God and I will beautify him" (Exodus 15:2), it will be as if we are pointing to Him, as is stated in the Midrash (*Exodus Rabbah* 23:19).

After a person has cultivated this approach, it culminates not in the self or any physical pursuit or aspiration, but in surrender. After a person has done everything he can do, he asks *Hashem* to show him the path. Everything has become illuminated.

At first, we [the students of the Rebbe] were unable to grasp the full intent of our master's thinking, but after some time, Providence again allowed us to hear these very teachings from our master's holy mouth, as well as additional comments and explanations. The Rebbe strongly adjured us to follow this practice.

This practice, in which a person lets go of his self by letting go of his thoughts and desires by the device of simply observing them, can enable the cultivation of whatever he thinks will be most beneficial to him and the world. It is a practice that anyone can engage in at any time, as long as he takes the time and makes the commitment.

About the Author

Rabbi BENJAMIN EPSTEIN, Ph.D. is an experienced psychologist, author, and speaker who blends traditional Mindfulness-Based Cognitive Therapy (MBCT) with cognitive behavioral, spiritual, and acceptance techniques. Dr. Benjy works effectively across a broad spectrum of age groups to enhance well-being by teaching how to live more mindfully and in the present. In addition to his private practice and mindfulness seminars, he spends his summers as the Director of Staff Development and Clinical Research in Camp HASC. Dr. Benjy is blessed to live in Jerusalem with his wife and four beautiful children. To find out more about Dr. Benjy visit his website at www.beginnersmind.co.